The Ghost & I

Scary Stories
For Participatory Telling

Edited by
Jennifer Justice

○ Yellow Moon Press ○
Cambridge, Massachusettes

ISBN: 0-938756-37-0

Production & Design by Robert B. Smyth

Photographs by Susan Wilson
        Camera Work Studio
        33 Richdale Avenue
        Cambridge, MA 02140
        (617) 547 -5457

Music Notation by Paul D. Lehrman

Editorial Interns: Douglas Toft & Mary Furlong

We are grateful to the following for permission to reprint their
material:
"The Ghost's Gold" & "The Ghost's Song" © 1991 Heather Forest
"The Woman in Grey" © 1985 Sheila Daily
"The Graveyard Voice" © 1985 Betty Lehrman
"Old Man Daniker" © 1987 Jay O'Callahan
"The Witch Song" © 1982 Bonnie Lockhart

Yellow Moon Press
P. O. Box 1316
Cambridge MA 02238
(800) 497 - 4385

Yellow Moon Press publishes and distributes over 500 books and audio
tapes of the best in contemporary storytelling resources available
today. Our 88 page catalog is **free**. Call or write for your copy.

To the memory of
Willa Pinkston Jones Justice
who made a beautiful witch on Halloween.

CONTENTS

A WORD ABOUT CREDITING SOURCES

There is often concern and question about crediting sources when using material from a collection like **THE GHOST AND I.** Thus, we are including the following guidelines.

1. The authors have implicitly given permission for you to tell their stories by agreeing to have them included here. Along with their permission comes the serious obligation for you, the teller, to credit them—both the author and the book—each time you tell the story.

2. You are <u>not</u> given permission to include the stories in any books, publications, or recordings, audio or video, without first obtaining permission from the author and the publisher. The authors' addresses are included in the "Notes on Contributors" section on page 125 should you need to contact an author about this.

These guidelines are easy to follow and important in that we all need to credit where our material comes from.

INTRODUCTION

Ghost stories are a universal favorite, found in cultures around the world. Ask any child what she/he wants to hear, and the inevitable answer will be: "Tell me a ghost story!" But, what exactly are ghost stories, and what makes them so popular?

Most of us recall our childhood ghost stories. I have a vivid memory of being on the screened porch in Grayton Beach, Florida. I must have been ten years old, one of the most popular ages for ghost stories. It was ten o'clock at night, a thrilling time to be awake. The adults—aunts, uncles, second cousins, great aunts and third cousins twice removed—were gathered downstairs playing duplicate bridge. Scattered about in the screened porch bunk beds were my sister and brother, and about ten assorted cousins. Bobby, Donny, and Billy had flashlights on their faces, giving them an eerie skeletal appearance. My cousin, Bobby, spoke in a hoarse whisper, his face scrunched into an unrecognizable mask, "Once there was a murder. Right here in Grayton Beach. It was horrible and gory...."
"Don't tell it!" I shrieked. Then clapped my hand over my mouth as everyone "schushed" me. Bobby went on with his tale as I huddled close under my older sister's protective arm.

Looking back, I wonder why I stayed on that porch night after night, listening to stories that my cousins invented or repeated. They were almost unbearably terrifying, yet how I loved them! All my favorite scary characters appeared at one time or another: witches, skeletons, vampires, and, of course, ghosts.

The quest for ghost stories usually begins around the age of five, when a child first acquires a concept of time: past, present, and, most challenging, future. I remember being driven in a car to kindergarten class with a group of friends. I don't know what the mother at the wheel was saying, but it provoked in me the realization that people die. I was dumbfounded! My mind was filled with wonderment and a million questions. If people died, where did they go? Could they come back? What happened to their bodies? Would my grandmother die? She was the oldest person I knew.

I began to dream of witches. They seemed to be the most powerful of the spirits that dealt with the question of death. They were wonderful, because they had no fear. They could make things happen. Most especially, they could fly on broomsticks across the moon.

In my many years of traveling about the country as a storyteller, I have noticed some important factors in telling ghost stories to children five to eight years old. The scariness must come in moderation, with a definite guarantee that all will turn out well. I also recommend including a certain amount of fun along the way. These were the ingredients I searched for in the ghost stories for younger children in this volume.

In the first section of **THE GHOST & I** younger children will meet brave girls who dare to go out searching for a ghost on Halloween night (THE GHOST HUNT and THERE'S NO SUCH THING). They will encounter mysterious graveyard food (GRAVEYARD VOICE), and giant, though impolite, pumpkins (STORY OF A PUMPKIN). Along the way there is a cat who overcomes his night fears (MY CAT IS AFRAID OF THE DARK). They will even encounter a witch who is foiled by her own evil plans (WITCH CRACKED UP). All of these stories for younger children include the important elements of humor and a happy ending.

By the time I was nine years old, I had discovered a love of using my wits to out-trick the ghosts and monsters. For Halloween I was dressing as skeletons and devils, because I was powerful enough to conquer them. My mother made herself a wonderful witch costume and answered the door for trick-or-treaters with a wild, wicked cackle. I loved the excitement of skirting danger in the dark as we tromped from door to door, returning safely home to hot chocolate and popcorn by the fire.

In the section of ghost stories for nine-to eleven-year olds, I looked for stories that still contained an element of humor. However, the humor involves the great tricks that overcome the somewhat scarier ghosts, such as a poor serving man who convinces the ghost of his former master that he is dead; or a simple tailor who outraces a monster. Children this age are ready to confront their fears and vanquish them.

In the second section of **THE GHOST & I**, children nine to eleven years old will find a haunted house with a treasure in the cellar (THE GHOST'S GOLD), a Scots tailor who braves monsters on a lonely heath at night (THE SPRIGHTLY TAILOR), and talking animals with seemingly cruel designs on a traveler (WAIT TIL MARTIN COMES). After we struggle with nasty witches (WITCHES ON A MOUNTAIN), we will discover that witches are actually a much maligned and misunderstood group of powerful men and women (WITCH SONG). A baker, a butcher and a blacksmith make a bargain with the devil in the old Grimm's tale, THE THREE APPRENTICES. Finally, from the Appalachian mountains comes a fantasy of riding with witches and robbers (UNCLE BILL'S DREAM).

In all of these stories, the children will find that they have the courage and the wit to win over their greatest fears. These ghosts are no match for them!

By the time I had reached the age of twelve, I spurned the simple answers. I knew that there were great mysteries to the universe, and I was more concerned with contemplating them than with answering them. There was also sadness in the world, and I wanted to know if there was anything I could do to help make things right.

The stories in the final section reflect these burgeoning mature concerns. It is the mystery of life that is at the center of these ghost story legends, rather than the humor to laugh at witches, or the courage to conquer fears.

In this third section we will encounter spirits who are trying to solve their sorrows, and humans who help them along their way. Of course, sometimes it is the spirits who help the humans, and those will be found here as well.

The stories in this last section are meant to be told as if they were true, and this sense of reality brings the warning or sorrow home to the heart. A mysterious mother begs a bottle of milk from a grocer in THE WOMAN IN GREY. An eerie legend from Japan combines the endless struggle for artistic freedom with vanquishing a terrifying monster (THE BOY WHO DREW CATS). From the Native American tradition comes a story of a mother's fight for life against a blood sucking skeleton (THE VAMPIRE SKELETON). Returning to the oriental tradition, we are posed an unanswerable question from the spirit world (SENJO). The final two stories of the collection (THE VANISHING HITCHHIKER and OLD MAN DANIKER) sit squarely in the tradition of the urban legend by establishing a strong sense of time and place for their haunting visitations.

In all of the stories in the third section, the listeners will discover their longing to contemplate the mysteries of life and death, and the ability to empathize, even with the struggles of ghosts.

The three sections of **THE GHOST & I** provide a perfect overview of the source of our ageless love of ghost stories. Whether it is for the fun of seeing ghosts revealed as silly and powerless, for the pride at our courage in outwitting them, or for our empathy in trying to help them—people have always loved ghosts!

A BRIEF HISTORY OF GHOSTS, ETC.

The fascination of ghost stories, at any age, comes from the thrill of toying with our fears and the satisfaction of conquering them. There is also a pure delight in contemplating the mystery of life and death. This contemplation has been going on among children and adults throughout the ages. What is the history of the ghost story?

The original ghost stories were tied to religious rites. Many people believed, and many still believe, that, under certain circumstances, the spirit stays around after the body dies. This spirit is usually trying to resolve some painful dilemma surrounding their death. Helping them resolve this problem is rewarded. Getting in the way is dangerous.

The word *ghost* derived from the same root as the Germanic word *geist* or *guest*. This reflects the tradition of inviting the spirit of a dead ancestor to tribal feasts and other solemn ceremonies. Today, in some parts of England, the words *ghost* and *guest* are still pronounced the same. In many stories you will find that the anger of the ghost is only evoked if one neglects to treat them with the respect accorded to a guest.

Some European people saved a seat at their table for their departed loved one, and put that loved one's skull at their place. The skulls would be given elaborate decoration and consulted for important advice. This explains the tradition of the carved pumpkin head on Halloween.

Witches have long been a slandered, persecuted group of people, providing stories with delicious fright. The word, *witch*, was translated from the Hebrew, *kasaph*, which means "seer" or "diviner." Through the ages witches have been women who were perceived to have special powers, whether to cure the sick, turn iron into gold, or one poor woman who was murdered for being able to ride a board on the waves in the sea.

Women branded with this name faced horrors ranging from loss of property to burning at the stake. In some countries during the Middle Ages, entire towns lost their population of women to the persecution of witches. Ironically, the fate of a witch often depended on her fortune, the wealthier witches receiving forgiveness if not outright acceptance, and the poorer being subject to the worst forms of retribution.

Because blood is essential to life, people believed, from the time of Homer, that the dead craved blood to make themselves live again. Hence, the Vampire. Since a belief in the power of the moon to call forth forces of life has also existed for centuries, it was inevitable that the full moon would be linked to the appearance of this special demon.

Ghosts, pumpkins, witches, and vampires—from every page of the book, we bring you an assortment of creatures, both good and evil, who will thrill your audiences and hold them captive when you invite them to participate in **THE GHOST & I**.

PARTICIPATION

From the first stories, when people created language to share the events of their days or to explain the mysteries of the universe, audiences have been helping the teller create the story. This help may come through actual suggestions in response to a question from the teller, or through creating the sounds of wind and rain. Sometimes the participation occurs simply as a responsive light in the listener's eye that lets the storyteller know an image has reached the heart.

Consciously eliciting participation, controlling it, and nurturing it along are all part of the art of the storyteller. Through the three sections of **THE GHOST & I**, storytellers will strengthen their ability to enjoy inviting an audience to take part in the storytelling.

Whether the participation is physically active or in the imagination, being part of a storytelling event brings an audience closer together. Storytelling creates community. This is its principle function and effect.

The lessons I have learned in participatory storytelling have been taught by my audiences. Children know better than anyone else when they would like to join in the story. They have taught me how to run through the forest with Coyote and how to fly through the air like Eagle.

I remember one of my early experiences as a professional storyteller. I had a new story, the traditional African story of Anansi the Spider who climbs to the sky and wins the story box from the Sky God. Like many storytellers, I develop a story through telling it to my audience, but this trial by fire was happening in front of a review board for a granting organization that could help me to get work in public schools. I was a bit nervous.

I was also new to audience participation. So, I started telling the story, without any active audience involvement. But, the second time Anansi climbed into the sky, the entire group of third and fourth graders hooked their thumbs together and wiggled their fingers high in the air. *I joined them* in the action. In unison we decided that it would be fun to make a shrill trilling noise as we raced from the sky back to earth. After that, it was a piece of cake.

This was both an exhilarating and an educational experience. I discovered that audiences *love* to be part of the story. With just the slightest permission, they will enthusiastically join in the telling. This is the most important thing for storytellers who are new to participation to remember. Your listeners will not need much encouragement, they are eager to take part. So, be fearless, and have fun.

THE BASICS OF PARTICIPATION

First, what kinds of things should a storyteller look for in a story involving participation?

1. **Repetition** - Anything that happens more than once in a story—a phrase of dialogue, an action, a sound, or the weather—can be learned quickly and easily by an audience.

2. **Actions** - When a character climbs into the sky, shakes a finger in a monster's face, or runs through a swamp, these actions invite participation. It is even better if the actions happen more than once, i.e., repetition.

3. **Sounds** - When opening a door, why not give it a rusty hinge? "Creeeaaak." If something falls suddenly to the ground, why not invite the audience to slap their hands and cry "Bump!" If the sound happens more than once, even better, i.e., repetition!

4. **Weather** - This is a favorite form of audience participation. Is there a storm? Let's make the wind howl and the thunder clap. Snap your fingers or slap your knees to make the rain fall. If it happens more than once....

5. **Anticipation** - When a word, or piece of action, is so predictable that an audience actually knows what is going to happen next, they can join you in making it happen. This occurs often with predictable, well-loved plots such as "The Three Little Pigs" and "Cinderella." Be aware when such a moment is about to occur and make room for audience to say with you, "But the shoe did not fit!"

6. **Questions** - This is a brave form of participation, since you must be ready for whatever answers come. However, it can be very fun to let the audience help you decide what happens next. Be prepared to politely, lovingly cut short the kindergartner who answers a question with a long story about how she "had a pumpkin once . . . " I interrupt her with a delighted, "That's wonderful. Will you tell me about it after I finish the story?" And continue my narrative.

7. **Empathy** - Where can your audience identify with the characters in the story? These are places to invite direct empathy with a phrase such as, "I don't know if this has ever happened to you" or simply to be aware that what your audience is feeling may carry them deeper into your tale.

8. **Ritual Phrases** - Many cultures have phrases that may be found in most of their stories. The most common such phrases in the Western European culture are "Once upon a time," and "They all lived happily ever after." These, and others, are wonderful opportunities for your listeners to join you. If you are telling a story from a culture that is less known to your listeners, teach the ritual phrase before you begin telling.

9. **Musical Instruments and Other Props** - Listeners may be invited to do everything from holding the "story stone" to banging on a drum when the thunder roars. Props and musical instruments are great, more directly personal ways to involve individual audience members in your story.

10. **Active Listening** - Children today spend so many hours in front of television screens, which require very little attention and usually invite no active involvement, that their ability to give full focus to anything is largely underdeveloped. Stories that draw them in through their imaginations and bring them to a point of total involvement, promote active listening skills that teach empathy, memory, verbal

structuring, story elements, and just about anything else you want to teach. All it takes is engaging their lively attention.

Once you have identified the types of participation available in your story, the next step is to learn the skills needed to successfully involve your audience in helping you tell the story.

THE "HOW TO" OF PARTICIPATION

There are three steps to audience participation:

1. **Teach It** - Most participation is simple enough to be taught as it occurs in the story. Participation only needs to be taught as part of the introduction to the story when it is complicated enough to interrupt the flow of your telling, or when it is loud enough to require sound level controls.

2. **Time It** - It is common for tellers to forget that their audience doesn't know when to stop participating. One way to let them know is to establish a definite number of times for the participation to occur. This can be done simply through modeling (i.e., if you clap your hands three times, they will understand to only clap their hands three times). Or by directly telling them: "We will say the magic word three times." Most of the time, modeling the timing will suffice. They will be watching you carefully, so if your timing is clear, theirs should follow.

3. **Control It** - Participation is a nightmare if it gets out of hand. With a small audience the timing established should be enough to control sound levels and frequency. However, with a larger audience you may want to establish some gestures for sound levels and stop signals. I will sometimes tell my audience: "I am the orchestra leader and you are the orchestra. When I raise my hands in the air, it's time for the storm. When I bring my hands down, it's time for the quiet. Let's practice."

If you follow these three "How To" steps, look for the ten types of participation, and enjoy discovering the story with your audience, you should have a wonderful time.

The most important thing to remember is that, whether the participation is active or in the quality of their listening, a story is always created in community. The way an audience responds to a story does, and should, effect the telling. That is the true source of the magic of storytelling.

Jennifer Justice
October 1992

For me storytelling is like a wave in the ocean; the teller and the listeners ride it together. With children five to eight years old, it is very easy to get them to jump on to the wave; the challenge is in controlling the ride.

Participation with younger children is at its most active, and guided activity is the best form of crowd control with this age group. They will follow the simplest hand movements whether you intend them to or not. The stories in this section take full advantage of this enjoyment.

We begin with a song, "Hi Ho for Halloween" which is easy to sing and teaches some American Sign Language through the repetitive movements. This is a great way to begin a show of ghost stories, because it is fun and the younger children catch on quickly that you are not going to scare them too much.

The stories that follow the song are filled with participation. Several of them give you something to do with every line. The young children will be so involved in helping to tell the story, they will never think to start a conversation with their neighbor about how they "have a cat who got lost in a graveyard once."

In these stories, you will find classic examples of the participation techniques: repetition, action, sound, questions, empathy, anticipation, props, active listening, and weather.

Hi Ho For Halloween

♩ = 146

Em
Hi, ho, for Hal – low – een,

D
When the witch – es all are seen, I

Em
won – der what this all could mean, Hi,

D **Em**
ho, for Hal - low een_____!

Hi, ho, for Halloween,
When the witches all are seen,
I wonder what this all could mean,
Hi, ho, for Halloween!

Making New Verses

Sing the first verse, then say, "What other things, besides witches, can you see on Halloween?" Choose someone whose hand is raised, and put their suggestion in the song: "Jonathan says, 'ghosts.' Let's put it in the song." Sing:

> Hi, ho, for Halloween,
> When the ghosts all are seen,
> I wonder what this all could mean,
> Hi, ho, for Halloween!

Repeat as desired, incorporating other "Halloween sights."

Movements

These movements are based on American Sign Language (ASL), although they are *not* actually ASL. Sing the song, demonstrating the movements:

WORDS	GESTURE
Hi,	Put one palm up, as though gesturing "I don't know."
ho,	Add the second hand in the same gesture.
for Halloween,	To sign, "Halloween:" make a "mask" by forming a diamond with both index fingers touching and both middle fingers touching. Hold the mask in front of your eyes, then separate your hands, simultaneously bringing the index and middle fingers of each hand together.
When the witches	Outline the triangle of a "witches' hat" by touching together the tips of all fingers above your head and then separating your hands, bringing them down in a slanting movement.
all are seen,	Sign "see" by extending the index and middle fingers of each hand, then holding them in front of your eyes—as if your finger tips could see. Direct your fingers as though they are looking up at flying witches.
I wonder what this all could mean,	Gesture "I don't know" by holding both palms up at your sides and shrugging your shoulders. Let your face look puzzled. For musicality, bounce your arms four times slightly in time to the beat.
Hi, ho, for Halloween.	Repeat the gestures for these words, above.

You can combine making new verses with movements. Here are some gestures for a few likely Halloween sights:

WHAT'S SEEN	GESTURE
ghost	Sign "spirit" by holding the index finger of one hand on the open, horizontal palm of the other, then raising the index finger in a wiggly vertical line—as though tracing smoke rising from your palm.
monster, goblin, etc.	Hold both partly clenched hands up at shoulder level, as though they were the claws of something scary.
vampire, Dracula	Show "fangs" by holding the bent index fingers of both hand in front of your teeth.

For other "sights," ask if anyone present knows sign language; if not, ask your group to think of an appropriate gesture.

Background of The Song

This song is adapted from a Scots Halloween folksong, traditionally sung by "guisers" (the Scots equivalent of "trick or treaters") who would go "thigging" (begging from door to door).

I learned it first from F. Marian McNeill's **HALLOWEEN: ITS ORIGIN, RITES AND CEREMONIES IN THE SCOTTISH TRADITION** (Edinburgh, The Albyn Press, n.d.).

The Ghost Hunt

Introduction

Storyteller: Let's create an eerie place of sights and sounds. Please say after me. "I hear the screeching owl."
Audience: I hear the screeching owl.
Storyteller: Hoo-hoo, hoo-hoo.
Audience: Hoo-hoo, hoo-hoo.
Storyteller: I hear the howling wolf.
Audience: I hear the howling wolf.
Storyteller: Oof oof oof OOOOOL.
Audience: Oof oof oof OOOOOL.
Storyteller: I hear the night raven.
Audience: I hear the night raven.
Storyteller: Aaw Aaw Aaw Aaw! Aaw Aaw Aaw Aaw!
Audience: Aaw Aaw Aaw Aaw! Aaw Aaw Aaw Aaw!

NARRATIVE	AUDIENCE RESPONSE OR TELLER'S ACTION
Let's go walking through the woods. Let's staaay together.	In a Dracula-type voice.
You never know what you might see or hear.	
Place your hands on your laps and say after me.	Natural voice
Not too fast.	Storyteller sets tempo. Slapping hands on thighs. Audience joins in.
Not too slow.	Audience will SAY and DO everything the storyteller does from now on. If they are hesitant to join in, you may encourage them with a nod of your head.
1-2-3-.	Audience repeats.

13

Heeeere we go!

Audience repeats.
etc.

We're going on a Ghost Hunt.
We're going on a Ghost Hunt.
ST-OP!

Sudden. Looking to the left.

LOOK!

Facial expression of surprise. Points to the left.

Wooooooooooo!

Slow, steady, deliberate, gradually building. Wiggling fingers.

I see a crooked tree!

Shoulders hunched, arms, hands, fingers spread out and bent like a crooked tree.

We can't go under it.

Mime with hands and arms a "going under" motion.

We can't go around it.
WHAT SHOULD WE DO?

Mime "going around."

Seeks an answer from a volunteer. Waits for appropriate answer, "climb it".

Let's go! Huf huf huf huf!
Huf huf huf huf! Huf huf huf huf!

Storyteller and audience say this together. Arms and hands reaching up, climbing motion. Voice gradually getting higher in pitch , as arms go higher and higher.

We're going on a Ghost Hunt!

Audience continues repeating words of the storyteller.

We're going on a Ghost Hunt!

With confidence. Steady beat of hands slapping thighs.

ST-OP!

Looking to the right.

LOOK!

Facial expression of surprise. Pointing to the right.

Wooooooooooooo!

Slow, steady, delicate, gradual building. Wiggling fingers.

I see a *muddy swamp*.

> Emphasis on "muddy swamp." Facial expression of disgust.

We can't go under it.

> Mime with hands and arms a "going under" motion.

We can't go around it.

> Hands and arms mime "going around."

WHAT SHOULD WE DO?

> Seeks answer from volunteer. "Swim it."

Let's go! Slush slush slush slush slush slush slush slush slush.

> Hands flapping in swimming movements.

We're going on a Ghost Hunt!

> Sing-song chant up the scale.

We're going on a Ghost Hunt!

> Like carefree happy children.

ST-OP!

> Looking straight ahead.

LOOK!

> Expression of surprise. Points ahead.

Woooooooooo!
I see a *huuuuuge corn field*.

> Arms and hands mime parting some corn stalks, head lifting up, looking over the top of the stalks.

We can't go under it.

> Hands and arms mime "going under."

We can't go around it.
WHAT SHOULD WE DO!

> Mime "going around."
>
> Volunteer answer, "go through it."

Let's go! SWISH! SWISH! SWISH! SWISH! SWISH! SWISH! SWISH! SWISH! SWISH!

> Sliding arms back and forth. Speaking together.

We're going on a Ghost Hunt!

> Peppy, cheerful, shoulders swaying as hands slap laps.

ST-OP!

> Looking straight ahead.

LOOK!

> Pointing very slowly and hesitantly. Face is uneasy.

Wooooooooooooo!
I see an iron gate.
We can't go under it.

> Mime "going under" motion.

We can't go around it.

> Mime "going around."

Do you want to open it?

Let's open it very very slooooooowly.
EEEEEEEEEEEEEEEEEEEEEEEEEEEEEK!

We're going on a Ghost Hunt.

We're going on a Ghost Hunt.
ST-OOOOOOOOP!
LOOOOOK!
WOOOOOOOOO!
I see a big.......
BIG!

BIIIIIIIIIIIIIG!

HOU--------SE!

We can't go under it.
We can't go around it.
DO YOU WANT TO GO IN IT?

The door is open. It's dark in there. Let's walk quietly
on our tippy toes. Sssssssssssssssssssh!
Tip-tip-tip-tip.
We're going on a Ghost Hunt.
I'm not afraaaaaaid.
Tip-tip-tip-tip.

Uuew!

I feel some sticky fingers!

I feel a long slimy arm!

Listen to different answers from audience.	
Storyteller and audience do this together while making "opening" motion.	
Looking cautiously around.	
Very slowly.	
Amazement.	
Gradually building up.	
Louder.	
VERY VERY LOUD! Arms extending outward.	
Pause before saying "house." They are expecting to hear "ghost" and will enjoy the surprise.	
"Going under" motion.	
"Going around" motion.	
Listen for various answers.	
Audience repeats only the "Sssssssssssssh!"	
Audience repeats.	
Slowly and quietly.	
Whispering.	
Continue tip-toe motion with fingers.	
Audience continues to repeat.	
Sudden stop. Jumping. Shaking.	
Stretch fingers out. Feel each stretched out finger slowly and carefully.	
Hand feels outstretched arm.	

I feel a thick thick neck.

Hands carefully feel neck.

I FEEL A (pause) GREAT BIG (pause) HEAD!

Loud! Hands carefully feel head.

TWO COLD EYES!

LOUDLY! Both hands feel eyes carefully.

A GOOEY NOSE!

Looking disgusted. Both hands feel nose very carefully.

A BIG MOUTH!

Looking very uncomfortable, wide-eyed.

TWO SHARP TEETH!

Whining or wailing. Each word emphasized and said loudly and slowly.

IT------
IS------
A------

Slowly and loudly.

G--H--O--S--T!

Screams loudly!

Audience is welcome to join in the screaming.

RRRRRRUUUUUUNNNNNNN!

Hands slapping thighs very rapidly.

Run through the house.

Audience continues to repeat WORDS and GESTURES.

Very fast pace.

RRRRRRUUUUUUNNNNNNN!
Open the gate. EEEEEEEEEEEEEK!

Shouting very loudly.

Motion of opening the gate.

RRRRRRUUUUUUNNNNNNN!
Go through the corn field!
SWISHSWISHSWISHSWISHSWISHSWISH!

Very fast. Sliding hands and arms back and forth.

RRRRRRUUUUUUNNNNNNN!
Swim the swamp!

Fast!

SLUSHSLUSHSLUSHSLUSHSLUSHSLUSH!

Tongue hanging out, out of breath. Hands flapping very quickly in swimming movements.

RRRRRRUUUUUUNNNNNNN!

Slapping thighs quickly!

Climb the tree!

HUFFHUFFHUFFHUFFHUFFHUFFHUFFHUFF!

Fast. Arms and hands reaching up, climbing motion.

RRRRRRUUUUUUNNNNNN!

Open your door. Lock it. Jump in bed. Go to sleep.

Narration is so fast here that the audience just mimes the actions without repeating the words.

DID THAT GHOST GET YOU?

Various audience responses.

OR DID <u>YOU</u> GET THAT GHOST!?

HAHAHAHAHAHAHAHAHAHAHAHAHA
HAHAHAHAHAHAHAHAHAHAHAHAHA!

Hysterical, witchy laughter.

NOTES

This story originated from the traditional BEAR HUNT story. It has been in the oral tradition, especially in the southeast, for most of this century. Its popularity is distinctly connected to the high level of participation involved in the telling, and the competition over who can go the fastest in the surprise reverse ending. Linda Goss developed it specifically as a fun story to tell at Halloween for children eight years and younger.

ADAPTED BY
BETTY LEHRMAN

The Graveyard Voice

NARRATIVE

AUDIENCE RESPONSE OR TELLER'S ACTION

This is a traditional story, and I'm going to need some help from you. We're going to set the scene, create the atmosphere through sounds. The first thing we need is the sound of the wind blowing through the trees. It goes like this... *whssssshh...*   Then we need the sound of the leaves skittering along the ground. You know how in the fall the leaves get really dry and crunchy, and as the wind blows they rustle. It sounds like this, *tch tch pt ptp tch tch....* And last of all we need the sound of a scary voice. And the voice says, "turn me over, turn me over!"

Wave arms as 'the wind' accompanying the sound effects.

Wave fingers to show leaves skittering.

Cup hand to mouth; make 'scary,' reverberating voice.

There was once an ordinary man named John, who lived with his beautiful wife Mary who was also — ordinary. And they had two wonderful children, Jimmy and Jeannie, who, truth to tell, were also... ordinary. In fact, the only extraordinary thing about this whole family was that they lived next door to a... graveyard.

Pause, then cup hands to face on 'graveyard'.

And every day, John would walk to and from work through the... graveyard. He could have walked around the graveyard, by the road, but that would have taken twenty minutes more. So ordinarily he walked through the graveyard and ordinarily this was no problem. Until one day.

It was late October, and you know what happens in late October, right? Yes, Halloween. And have you ever noticed that on Halloween it gets really dark really early? That's not your imagination; it's true.

Really ask question and respond to whatever answers they come up with.

Because we turn back the clocks an hour the weekend before Halloween. So all of a sudden it's dark a whole hour earlier.

Well, it was late October, just three days before Halloween. They'd just turned back the clocks so it was really dark when John left his office at his usual time, 5:30, to begin his walk home through the... graveyard. And just as he came to the graveyard gate, he heard the wind through the trees. And the leaves skittering along the ground. And then he heard a voice saying, "Turn me over, turn me over!" So he <u>ran</u> all the way home.

And when he got home ("whew"), he told his wife, Mary, and his children, Jim and Jeannie, what he'd heard in the graveyard and they laughed at him. "Hee he hee!"

"Dear," she said. "Daddy," they said, "there's nothing in the graveyard."

The second night, John left his office at his usual time, 5:30, to begin his walk home through the... graveyard. And again just as he came to the graveyard gate, he heard the wind through the trees. And the leaves skittering along the ground. And then he heard that voice saying, "Turn me over, turn me over!" So he <u>ran</u> all the way home.

And when he got there ("whew"), he told his wife, Mary, and his children, Jim and Jeannie, what he'd heard in the graveyard and again they laughed at him.

"Dear," she said. "Daddy," they said, "There's nothing in the graveyard."

The third night it was Halloween, and John was determined to find out what it was in the graveyard: he knew it was <u>something.</u> So he left his office at his usual time, 5:30, to begin his walk home through the... graveyard. And even before he came to the graveyard gate, clouds passed in front of the moon. It was pitch black.

He came to the graveyard gate, he heard the wind through the trees. And the leaves skittering along the ground. And then he heard that voice saying, "Turn me over, turn me over!"

Do wind and leaves actions & sounds

Cup hand over face; reverberating voice

Cover mouth with hand as if laughing

Wind & leaves motions & sounds

Cup hand over face; reverberating voice

Cover mouth with hand; children do 'he hee hee'

Children say "there's nothing in the graveyard" with teller

Children say '5:30' with teller; also 'graveyard,' with hand cupped to face

Wind & leaves sound & movement

Hand cupped; reverberating voice

He followed the sound of the voice, through some trees, past some bushes, down a path, until he came to the very center of the graveyard. And then he saw where the voice was coming from. It was a huge marble crypt, a stone tomb surrounded by a wrought iron fence. He put his hand on the fence gate and pushed it open. It cree-eeaked. Then he began to walk down the steps toward the entrance of that tomb. And as he walked he counted: there were 13 steps.

Mime pushing gate; children respond by joining in with the 'creak' sound

In front of him was a huge metal door. He could hear the voice coming from behind the door. It was saying, "Turn me over, turn me over!" He put his hand on the doorknob and turned it, cree-eak... and looked inside.

Hand cupped in front of face; reverberating voice

Children join 'creak'

(pause)

And there, on the floor of that tomb was a flaming pile of red hot coals. And on top of those coals was a metal grid. And on top of that grid was a.... hamburger, done on one side. So he picked up the spatula, and he turned the hamburger over. And it said, "thaaank youuuuu."

Hand cupped in front of face; children join in the 'thank you.'

NOTES

Betty first heard this story in the perfect traditional setting: at camp when she was nine years old. It has been making the camp circuit for at least that long, and been recorded on the page in many different versions befitting a story still being passed along by word of mouth. It is recorded on Betty's tape, *Tales for the Telling*.

ADAPTED FROM AN AFRICAN FOLKTALE BY
FRAN STALLINGS

The Story Of A Pumpkin

Introduction

This pumpkin story has obvious applications at Halloween or Thanksgiving. It also fits well into Spring units on plant growth and development. The suspense of the chase sequence makes it welcome at campfire-type tellings when young listeners demand "scary" stories but you'd rather not give them nightmares.

NARRATIVE	AUDIENCE RESPONSE OR TELLER'S ACTION
I'm going to tell you a story about a pumpkin. So first, I want you to think about the pumpkin you had for Halloween, or for Thanksgiving decorations. Now SHOW ME with your hands: how big was it? How high?	Hold your own hands apart at an average pumpkin height, maybe 10 inches. Look expectantly at audience, encouraging "Show me?" Look at their "pumpkins" appreciatively.
And how wide was it?	Again show an average diameter, maybe 12 inches, and ask "Show me?" Some of those pumpkins will be pretty impressive… Nod to show that you believe all of this.
Pumpkins come in all sizes. Some are very small .	Mime those teeny ones used for table decorations, about 2-3" diameter.
Some grow so big that they win a prize!	Stretch arms around a 300 pounder, diameter four feet!

But once there was a great big, huge, gigantic, enormous, humongous pumpkin.

Add your own synonyms for "big" stretching your arms further and further apart: humongous!

It was so big that it even had a name: "Feegbah", which means "Big Thing". Let me hear you say its name.

"Feegbah."

And what does it mean?

"Big Thing."

Right. But of course it didn't start out as a great big pumpkin. It started out as a little white seed.

You remember the seeds you found inside when you scooped out your pumpkin. The seeds were about this big. Lots of them, in all that pumpkin glop.

Finger and thumb about 1/2" apart.

You remember. Now check behind your ear and see if you still have one.

Incredulity! But go ahead: feel behind your own ear. Sure enough, you find one! Hold it up in triumph. They will start feeling for theirs.

We're going to plant our seeds. Have you got yours?

Even the skeptics generally find one now, sometimes several. If they don't find one behind their ears, suggest that they try in their hair.

This carpet* looks pretty clean but I think there's enough dirt here to plant a pumpkin. So, let's dig a hole.

* [floor tile; desk-tops etc.]

Mime digging with your hand. Nod encouragingly to those who mimic you. Everyone can grow these pumpkins!

Drop in the seed. Cover it up. Pat it down.

Mime these actions as you speak. Then wait, watching the spot. Begin to look puzzled and disappointed.

It's not growing! What does it need?

"WATER!" (For some reason the majority always think of Water before Sun.)

Okay, let's water it.

Mime pouring water from a container; make glugging noises. Wait

24

It's still not growing! What else does it need?
But we're inside. That's okay, WE can shine on it.

and watch. Look more puzzled and disappointed.
"SUN!"

Frame your face with your hands, fingers spread to form rays. Smile innanely to "shine" down on the planted seed.

That did it! It's growing!
We can show how it grows. Use your one hand for the ground and the other for the little sprout. It's growing!

Hold one hand horizontal, fingers together . Poke fingertip of other hand up between two closed fingers.

And it grew bigger

Extend finger further through.

… and bigger

Make that two fingers extending through.

… and it grew into a vine

Extend whole hand, then forearm through.

… and the vine twined around

Wave hand and forearm sinuously.

… and it grew until there came a

Open hand, extend fingers radially

…. flower! And along came a

Making a buzzing noise, use the "ground" hand now to bumble along to the flower.

… bee.

Bumble the bee in the flower, then fly it away.

Because flowers have to have a bee.

[No further comment on sex education.]

And then the flower wilted,

Flop flowerhand over limply on wrist.

and where it used to be there was a teeny, green, little baby pumpkin!

Make flower hand into a tight fist.

And the baby green pumpkin grew bigger

Expand fist a bit.

… and bigger

Spread fingers as if enclosing a tennis ball.

… and bigger

Spread fingers to enclose half a larger ball, adding second hand to hold the other half. As the pumpkin grows, make your voice more excited and louder.

… and bigger

Separate your hands, spreading fingers wider.

… and bigger, bigger, **bigger**

Spread hands, then arms, wider and wider

…. and it turned yellow; and it turned orange; and it turned into Feegbah! Which means -- ?

"Big Thing!"

Now one day Feegbah was sitting on the pumpkin hill in the pumpkin patch, very happy and contented, when along came a kid about *your age* .

Arch arms to the side to show girth; grin smuggly.

Significant look at audience.

The kid saw that great big, huge pumpkin.

Now you step into character as the Kid. Step a pace to one side and stare agog at the spot Feegbah occupies.

"Wow! What a great big, huge, enormous, gigantic, humongous pumpkin! Just think how many pumpkin pies you could make out of that pumpkin! And pumpkin cake, and pumpkin bread, and…

Look to audience for advice and they will suggest other things, such as pumpkin cookies, roasted seeds, etc; you can add pumpkin soup, pumpkin ice cream. This is sounding better and better!

"But you can't make any of those unless the pumpkin is ripe. You can tell by the sound. Come on, let's knock on this pumpkin and see if it's ripe. Bip, bip, bip."

Tap gently against Feegbah's imaginary side. Audience will usually tap with you, sounds and all.

"Hey Kid! Don't do that! It tickles!"

Step back into Feegbah's space, arms arched, and glare at Kid's space looking very annoyed.

26

"Did I hear...? Nah, pumpkins don't talk. Come on, let's see if it's ripe. Bop, bop, bop."

Step back into Kid's space and stare puzzled at Feegbah. Exchange glances with audience. Tap harder.

Feegbah frowns and shudders in place.

Kid is dumbfounded.

"Hey Kid! Go away! You bother me!"

"Did I hear...? Nah, it couldn't be.
Pumpkins don't talk. Come ON, let's see if this
pumpkin is ripe. BAP, BAP, BAP!"

Tap very hard.

Now this made Feegbah so angry that that great big
pumpkin began to rock back and forth.

Mime actions as you describe them.

so hard that the vine broke, and Feegbah went rolling
down the pumpkin hill -- right after the Kid!

Teeter threateningly, then "break" loose and loom over audience. Cycle hand over hand in a forward wheeling motion. Nod encouragement to those in the audience who mimic this wheeling action, and others will join in.

The Kid started to run.

Pat your hands on your knees or thighs; audience will immediately mimic this. The only complication occurs if listeners are seated at desks or tables. Patting on those will make too much noise. Forestall that by directing, "Pat your knees to help the Kid run!" After you've got a good Running noise going, shift back to the Rolling gesture.

And Feegbah rolled.

They generally change over to this silent gesture without further prompting, allowing you to continue.

The Kid ran to the Forest. "Trees," said the Kid, "Feegbah
is after me! Please, please move aside so I can run
through!"

Wave your arms airily overhead: now you are a Tree. Nod encouragingly to kids who mimic this.

27

The Trees said, "Hmm, this is a very polite child. All right, we will move." The Trees moved to one side.

The Kid ran on through.

And the Trees moved back.
Feegbah came rolling,
and did not say please. Feegbah just rolled over those Trees, and made them flatter than... toothpicks! And the Kid kept running.
And Feegbah kept rolling.
The Kid ran down the road. There was a herd of Pigs, headed to market. "Pigs," said the Kid, "Feegbah is after me! Please, please move aside so I can run through!"

The Pigs said, "Hmm, this is a very polite child. All right, we will move." The Pigs moved to one side.
The Kid ran on through.
And the Pigs moved back.
Feegbah came rolling,
and did not say please. Feegbah just rolled over those Pigs, and made them flatter than... bacon!
And the Kid kept running.
And Feegbah kept rolling.
The Kid ran into the Town. "Houses," said the Kid, "Feegbah is after me! Please, please move aside so I can run through!"
The Houses said, "Hmm, this is a very polite child. All right, we will move." The Houses moved to one side.
The Kid ran on through.
And the Houses moved back.
Feegbah came rolling,
and did not say please. Feegbah just rolled over those Houses, and made them flatter than... paper! And the Kid kept running.
And Feegbah kept rolling.

Mince to one side, waving arms.

Brush one hand forward and the other back, clapping in the middle as they pass: whoosh.

Arms overhead again.

Wheel motion.

Pat knees.

Wheel.

Hunch over, make a piggy-face, grunt a little. Encourage audience to join you, "Come on, let's be pigs".

Waddle to one side, grunting amiably.

Whoosh as before.

Waddling.

Wheel motion.

Pat knees.

Wheel.

Hold angled arms overhead to make a roof.

Lumber to one side, arms overhead.

Whoosh as before.

Arms overhead again.

Wheel.

Pat knees.

Wheel.

The Kid ran back out into the country. There in the middle of the field was a herd of Cows. "Cows," said the Kid, "Feegbah is after me! Please, please help me!" The Cows said,"Hmm, this is a very polite child.

Lean forward, holding curved fingers to forehead for horns.

All right, we will help you. Come into our field and we will make a circle around you, with our horns pointing out. That is how we protect our calves from the wolves." So the Kid hid in the middle of the herd of Cows, and they waited with their horns pointing out.

Point your horns with bovine alertness.

Feegbah came rolling

Wheel.

right up to that herd of Cows. The Cows caught Feegbah on their horns and tossed that big pumpkin right up in the air!

As a Cow, catch something massive on your horns and toss it with satisfaction.

Feegbah turned over three times

Circle one hand high overhead.

and came down, Crash!, on the ground.

Mime impact, disintegration.

And Feegbah broke into two pieces. The big piece went up into the sky and became the big orange Sun.

Point overhead to one side and nod sagely, this certainly makes sense.

The smaller piece went up into the sky and became the big orange Moon.

Point overhead to the other side and nod. What, are there skeptics in the audience?

Haven't you seen the moon when it's rising with dust in the air? It's just as orange as a pumpkin!

Some will have seen this. Before they have time to ask how come a pumpkin-derived moon isn't orange all the time, continue:

And the little white seeds went up into the sky and became all the thousands and thousands of ...

Pause; somebody will surely exclaim: "STARS!! "

You are impressed by their logic.

So -- I guess it must be a true story!

Put on a goofy gullible look and nod, to share mutual awareness that only silly people would take this seriously. Sometimes somebody demands to know what happened to all the stringy gook inside the pumpkin. With luck somebody else will explain that this made the Clouds. And I guess the juice is Rain. So you see, it all works out.

NOTES

Follow-up Activities

CREATIVE DRAMATICS. After hearing this story, children five and up can readily improvise a skit from it. Don't bother with a script: the story is so patterned, they already know their lines. Do review the story's sequence first, for a comprehension check. Then cast individuals as Feegbah and Kid, and pick groups of Trees, Pigs, Houses, and Cows. When space (and soundproofing) allowed, I have involved up to 30 children. Let the Storyteller serve as Narrator the first time; someone else can take over later. Discuss the necessary scenes (pumpkin patch; forest; road; town; cow pasture) and decide where to locate them in the room. Everyone take your places; GO. They will want to switch roles and do it again. And again.

To avoid mayhem, here are some suggestions. Explain that this is all pretend, so there will be no actual contact when the Kid "taps" the Pumpkin; and when the Feegbah "rolls over" obstacles, she/he will merely pass among them as they flatten to the ground. Space is limited, so remind the "running" Kid to move in slow, mincing steps while patting knees. Feegbah walks sedately behind, "rolling" with the arm motion.

Sources and Related Tales

This story comes from Upper Volta (Guillot, René, **GUILLOT'S AFRICAN FOLK TALES**, selected and translated by Gwen Marsh. NY: Watts, 1965. pp 96-97.) The original text says the pumpkin was finally stopped by a herd of horned sheep, not cows; and its two halves made the sun and the sky (rather than the moon), seeds made stars, pulp made Milky Way.

I have not yet found other African or neighboring versions of this tale, but there is a Hawaiian creation myth about a calabash: top = sky, pieces = sun & moon, seeds = stars, remainder = earth. "Calabash" can refer to various squashes, gourds, pumpkins or to the fruit of a tropical American tree. This tale can be found in: Thompson, Vivian Laubach, **HAWAIIAN MYTHS OF EARTH, SEA, AND SKY**, (New York: Holiday, 1966, 11-14.)

I first heard this story from New York storyteller, Marcia Lane, who involved the audience in the Running, Rolling, and Whoosh gestures. I added the opening sequences (How big? Growth from a seed), the tapping sequence, and gestures for the Trees, Houses, Pigs, and Cows. In developing a skit from the story, I had help from dozens of K-2 classes with whom I have worked in State Arts Council of Oklahoma residencies.

FLORA JOY

The Witch Who 'Cracked Up'

Introduction

Audience members may participate in this story in two different ways. One group manipulates a set of tangrams for this story. These helpers will need to familiarize themselves with the shapes prior to your telling of the story. These tangram pieces may be enlarged if the helpers plan to face the listeners as they hold the pieces in the air. From four to seven helpers may be needed with these large pieces. Only one or two are needed to demonstrate the same idea with the use of an overhead projector. Before beginning this story, arrange the tangram pieces for the witch as shown on this page. The thin white lines appear only as clues to the arrangement of the shapes. **Squeeze the pieces together** for the storytelling. Further positioning instructions are provided during the story. The **second** method of audience participation (indicated in right columns with the label **Teller**) asks the listeners to make the witch noises as the story is told. All will cackle "E-brack-a de-hack-a" when the teller raises her/his arms. When the teller points to the audience, the listeners should cackle "Eh, eh, eh" until the pointing ceases.

NARRATIVE	AUDIENCE RESPONSE OR TELLER'S ACTION
Once there was a mean and ugly witch named Tanna. She was known throughout the land as the cruelest and most savage of all witches. Children fled in terror when they heard her cackle in the distance. The animals in the forest raced for safety whenever the door of her wretched little shack creaked open. All knew that each time Tanna raised her long bony arms and shouted "E-brack-a de-hack-a," another life would be ruined. As time passed, Tanna became more hideous and vile than ever. Daily she hunkered in the corners of her hut plotting and scheming new and even crueler spells to cast on others.	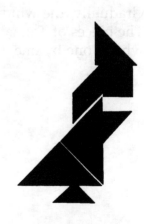 **Tangram Group:** If an overhead projector is used, have the tangram

31

pieces positioned for the witch. Turn it on soon after the teller begins the story. If a group is holding the enlarged pieces, they may show the witch as the teller begins the story.

Teller: Raise your arms high in the air as you say "E-brack -a de-hack-a," thus encouraging the listeners to say this with you.

One day she devised her meanest plan of all! This plan would slowly and painfully destroy all the people and all the animals in the land. The witch cackled in sadistic delight as she thought of her plan. "Eh, eh, eh, eh!"

Teller: Point to audience as you cackle, "Eh, eh, eh, eh!" They will cackle with you.

Teller: Raise arms as you say "E-brack-a de-hack-a."

Then she raised her bony arms and began her shrill incantations of doom, "E-brack-a de-hack-a." But suddenly out of nowhere a bolt of lightning surged from the dark sides and struck Tanna with such staggering force that her body cracked into many large pieces. The snapping and popping of that old witch's bones could be heard in the farthest corners of the forest. The winds hurled those witch chunks high into the air and continued to toss and batter them about without mercy.

Gradually, the winds died down and the storm ended. The pieces of Tanna's body slowly floated back to the earth where, one by one, they fell to the ground.

Tangram Group: Toss and swirl the seven tangram pieces "without mercy."

Continue this tossing and swirling until; you hear the words, **But the pieces didn't turn back into a witch. They became ... A CAT!** At this point, "settle" these pieces into the cat shape.

But the pieces didn't turn back into a witch. They became
. . . **A CAT!**

All of the other witches in the land saw what happened to
Tanna that night, and to this day they still remember the
lesson they learned. That is why at Halloween you never
actually see any real witches. But when you go trick-or-
treating, if you happen to hear something scampering
about on a front porch or scratching in the nearby bushes,
if it is making a low purring noise, it just might be
Tanna—in her cat form, of course. But never you fear, it
is no longer possible for Tanna to cast spells on anyone.
Nevermore will she be able to act upon her ugly thoughts
and chant "E-brack-a de-hack-a." In fact, all she will ever
be able to utter for the rest of her days is "meow."

Perhaps you should remember what happened to Tanna
the next time you have a cruel thought!

"Eh. . . Eh. . . Eh. . .

Eh. . . Ehm. . . Ehme. . . Ehmeow. . .

"Meow. . .Meow. . . Meow!"

Teller: Raise arms as
you say "E-brack-a de
hack-a."

Teller: Point to
audience as you say,
"Eh, eh, eh." but
gradually lower your
finger as you blend into
the "Meow."

NOTES

Tangram Information: A tangram is a Chinese puzzle made by cutting a square into
five triangles, a square, and a rhomboid. (See example on the next page.) The actual
origin of this puzzle is unknown. Some authorities explain the name of the puzzle as a
derivative of the word **t'ang** which means "Chinese." Others relate it to **tanka**, the
river dwellers with whom traders dealt in earlier days when the Chinese government
forbade communication with outsiders. Still others describe a Chinese man named
Tuan who dropped a square object which broke into seven pieces. As he tried to
reshape the original square, he discovered thousands of other shapes in the process.
You can recombine these shapes into many different figures, such as the "witch" and
the "cat" in this story. Have fun arranging these pieces into other patterns. As you do
so, however, please remember that the tangram craze has reportedly hit many
intellectuals. It is rumored that John Quincy Adams, Edgar Allen Poe, and Lewis
Carroll (just to name a few) caught tangram fever. **Beware, for there is no cure.**
For those who wish to provide audience members each with a set of tangrams, a
machine exists (Ellison Die machine) which cuts about a dozen sets per minute with
the tangram die. This machine can be located in the materials center of most school
systems.

TANGRAM EXAMPLE

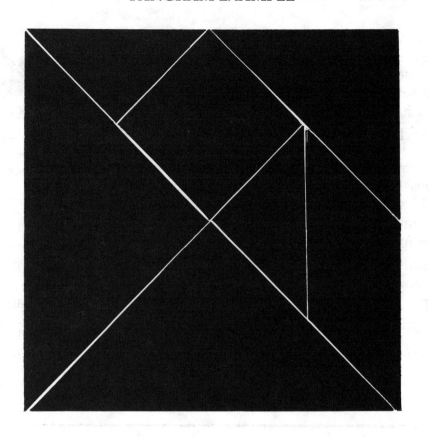

JULIA WILLIS

My Cat Is Afraid Of The Dark

Introduction

This is a story/poem that requires the teller to do some untraditional memorizing. The result is well worth the effort. You might begin by asking if anyone in your audience is afraid of the dark. Then teach them the repetitive phrase, "My cat is afraid of the dark." There is also a wonderful opportunity for participation near the end when the cat gets a scary mask. See how many scary faces your listeners can make.

NARRATIVE	AUDIENCE RESPONSE OR TELLER'S ACTION

When the sky is all covered
In peaches and cream,
And all that we hope
Can become what we dream,

When the sun goes to China
And pink clouds turn grey,
And the newscaster says
It's the end of the day,

My cat eats his tuna
And sits in his bath
And blow-dries his tail
Just to make himself laugh,
Then slips on his polka-dot
Paisley pajamas
And finds Wog and Woolly,
His favorite stuffed llamas --

And just as the stars
Join their hands 'round the night,
I read him a story
And tuck him in tight,

With his big fuzzy pillow,
His Woolly to hold,
And an extra blue blanket
In case he gets cold.

Yet no sooner am I
In a bed of my own
Than who should begin
To both whimper and moan
Till the neighbors complain
And their little dogs bark
But my cat --
Who's afraid of the dark.

My cat is afraid of the dark.

Signal the audience
that now is the time for
them to join in this
repetitive phrase.

Now it's not that he's timid
Or lacking in pluck,
For he loves to climb trees
And he never gets stuck.

In rainy day hallways
His courage abounds
Once he fought my umbrella
And won in three rounds.

On patrol in the garden
He covers all bases
And puts those wild butterflies
Right through their paces.

Under the beds
Where the dust bunnies roam
He rounds up the strays
And he herds them straight home.

So quick to respond
Yet so tender, you see,
That he'll catch his own tail
But he'll soon set it free.

So brave to a fault,
So easy to please,
So full of himself
Nearly everyone sees
That he's handsome and clever

With talents to spare,
Giving off the impression
He hasn't a care.

So how could you guess
That a cat so unique
Exceedingly hearty
And terribly chic
Would be any less
When I turn out the light
And let in the silence
That comes with the night?
But alas, it's no matter
He sings like a lark -
When my cat is afraid of the dark.

My cat is afraid of the dark.

Audience joins in again.

It's clear every morning
He's college material,
Just by the way
He eats up all his cereal.

Speaking in public
To birds flying south
Words of four syllables
Melt in his mouth.

He helps with the dishes
He wrings out the mop
And eats all his spinach
With catnip on top.

He speaks perfect Greek,
He's mastered French cooking,
And plays a mean sax
When he thinks no one's looking.

From tennis with turtles
To polo with newts,
He plays at more games
Than a lawyer has suits.

While in matters requiring
A smidgin of tact,
He'll sort out the issues
And call you right back.

As sweet as a kitten
As strong as a lion,
He quickly repels
Every negative ion.
Consistently growing
By leaps and by bounds,
He weighs ten big kilos
(Or twenty-two pounds).
Last week he went fishing
And reeled in a shark!

But still I confess --
He's afraid of the dark.

My cat is afraid of the dark.   Audience joins in.

If he's not up a flagpole
To hang by his thumbs,
He'll be off riding subways
When rush hour comes.

With derring and do,
With courage and cunning,
He's been to the moon
For six Saturdays running.

No one can deny
It's his style that prevails --
Why, he even goes dancing
In white tie and tails.

Yes, he's everything fine
That a feline should be,
Prouder and stronger
And smarter than me.
With never a blunder
And never a blush,
When he steps to the plate
O'er the crowd falls a hush,
Then he swings and the ball
Flies right out of the park --
So how could my cat be
Afraid of the dark?

My cat is afraid of the dark.   Audience joins in.

Oh, it's not a faint heart
Or a yellow-streaked spine

That turns him to Jello --
It's merely a sign
That the dark is a place
Where the mind runs the show
And the more he imagines
The worse worries grow.
For it's not what he sees
That supplies him such fright,
It's the things that he *can't* see
But fears he just *might*.

I've pondered this problem
So long and so deeply
That some of my own jangled
Nights have been sleep-free.

But here's a solution
To ease my cat's eyes
And cut phantom bloodsuckers
Right down to size:

It's not pulling covers
Up over his ears
To breathe through a straw
Much too thin for fat fears.

It's not making believe
If he shouts "ALCAZONY!"
A three-headed monster
Turns into a pony.

I'll make him the scariest
Mask in the world
With a hideous grin,
A nose long and curled,
Which my cat will strap on
To stare into the black
So that whatever scares him
He'll scare it right back!
With a growl in his throat
And a swipe of his claws,
In one mighty swoop
He'll find freedom because
Every google-eyed fiend,
Every demon by birth,
Will run screaming away

This is a great
opportunity for the
listeners to create their
own scariest masks and
put them on. They can
then help to scare the
monsters "right back!"

To the ends of the earth
Where they each will be eaten
By hungry cat clones,
Who'll feast on their flesh
And make soup from the bones!

Now the night is a time
When some cats find no peace,
Always batting at shadows
And screaming "POLICE!"

But it soon will be quiet
In his little room,
Once my cat sends his terrors
Back into the gloom.

For a soft breeze will whisper
Where curtains are hung
To soothe and caress
Like his mama's pink tongue

And the dark will encircle
With its sweet embrace
Dear cat, as his eyes
Blink "Good night" to his face.

Then we'll all sleep as soundly
As kittens in hay,
Knowing life's always grander
The very next day.

This is a classic bedtime story ending. Just right for tucking children into bed and sending them safely to sleep.

NOTES

It's not easy as children to feel powerful enough to stand up to our fears; many of us learned to breathe under the covers - we had so many opportunities to practice. Not only are we limited by our size, but adults are often so willing to assume we aren't capable of handling power (odd, when you consider the way so many adults abuse theirs). As a former child myself, I'd say bestowing and confirming power at a very young age is the best way of honoring a child and creating a fearless, responsible adult. That's what I was thinking when I wrote *My Cat*. And I used a cat character because, in my own experience, while a dog may bark at the faintest noise outside, it's the cats, in spite of their numerous accomplishments, who always see those quiet demons in the corner.

There's No Such Thing

Introduction

Since I'm a musician as well as a storyteller, I prefer to teach the songs as they occur in the story. This is simple and shouldn't interrupt the flow of the telling. However, if you are less comfortable with music, you may teach the audience to sing the songs as part of your introduction. If you aren't comfortable singing at all, the songs may be chanted.

Teaching the sounds of the owl, cat, dog, and wind is more complicated and should be done before you begin telling. I sometimes divide the audience into three parts for the owl, cat, and dog, assigning one sound to each group. The wind is done with the whole audience.

With a large audience, you may also want to introduce noise level controls. I will remind them that the sounds shouldn't hurt my ears or disturb people studying math in the next room. Hand signals can also set sound levels.

NARRATIVE	AUDIENCE RESPONSE OR TELLER'S ACTION
I knew it all along, I knew it all along, Don't you know, you can't fool me, I knew it all along.	Storyteller sings or chants the song.
Once, on Halloween night, a little girl was sitting at home with her family. Outside, under the full, orange, harvest moon, the owls hooted.	Invite the audience—either verbally or just by pausing and cupping your ear—to make hooting sound.
The cats meowed.	Audience makes sound.
The dogs howled.	Audience makes sound.
The wind wailed through the trees around the house.	Audience makes sound.
She went into her bedroom to get away from all the scary sounds. But her brother, who always teased her, was	

hiding behind her door. He jumped out and yelled, "Boo! I'm the Headless Ghost!"

The little girl shrieked.

Audience makes sound with previous coaching about how loud a shriek is permissible in your surroundings.

Her brother laughed, "Scared you, scared you, scared you!"

She said, "I'm not scared of anything."

Her brother said, "I bet."

She said, "I'll show you. I'm going to...take a walk outside."

Do you think that was a good idea? On Halloween? With the owls and cats and dogs and the wind making noises out there?

Storyteller asks this to audience, who will respond with mix of "yes's" and "no's."

Her brother said, "It's Halloween night! Don't you know what's out there? Goblins, and skeletons, and witches, and ... even the Headless Ghost."

The little girl said, "I'm not scared of anything."

She started walking down the street: step, step, step, step.

Audience joins in with "walking" of hands on legs, and saying "step, step, step...."

She heard someone else walking behind her. She slowed down, and the sounds slowed down.

Audience follows cues.

She went faster, and the sounds went faster.

She stopped, and the sounds stopped.

Audience stops

She was afraid to turn around. She was sure there was a goblin on the street, waiting to grab her.

So she made a little song, and sang it out loud:

    "There's no such thing."

Sing.

Under the full, orange, harvest moon, the owls hooted.

Audience hoots.

    "There's no such thing."

Around her, the cats meowed.

Audience meows.

    "There's no such thing."

The dogs howled

Audience howls.

    "As goblins."

The wind wailed through the trees.

Audience makes wind sound.

But, her song gave her courage. She stamped her foot.

She heard the sound of a foot stamping.

Audience stamps foot

She clapped her hands. She heard the sound of hands clapping.

Audience claps.

She said, "Is there an echo here?"

She heard, "Is there an echo here?"

Audience echoes.

It was no goblin, it was just an echo on that part of her street! She sang,

> "I knew it all along,
>
> I knew it all along,
>
> Don't you know, you can't fool me,
>
> I knew it all along."

Sing or chant.

She said, "I'm not afraid of anything. But maybe I won't walk on the street anymore."

Next to the street, there was a ditch. It had grass growing in it, and mud at the bottom. It was hard to see what else was in it.

The little girl said, "Maybe I'll walk...in the ditch."

Do you think that was a good idea? On Halloween night? I don't think it was. I don't know if you would do it. But she did.

Audience responds with "yes's" and "no's."

Her feet slurped through the mud in the ditch, "Slurp, slurp, slurp, slurp."

Audience makes "walking" motions and "slurp" sound.

All of a sudden, someone grabbed her foot! She pulled it loose, but someone grabbed her other foot.

She was afraid to look down. She was sure a skeleton was holding on to her foot.

But the little girl remembered her song:

> "There's no such thing... (etc)"

Sing; audience make sounds as before

The song made her feel brave enough to look down. Around her foot, there was a vine, growing in the ditch.

It hadn't been a skeleton, after all.

She said,

> "I knew it all along... (etc)"

Sing as before.

She said, "I'm not afraid of anything. But maybe I won't walk in the ditch anymore. Maybe I'll walk...in those dark woods over there."

Do you think that was a good idea? On Halloween night? I don't think so. I hope you wouldn't do it; but that's what she did.

Audience responds with "yes's" and "no's."

She walked on the crunchy leaves of the woods: crunch, crunch, crunch, crunch.

Audience makes "walking" motions and "crunch" sound.

All of a sudden, just five trees ahead of her, she saw a witch on a broomstick. It was bobbing up and down in the air. She heard a short, evil laugh. "Eeeh!"

She was so frightened, she was ready to run home, but she remembered her song:

"There's no such thing …(etc)"

Sing; audience makes sounds.

The song made her feel brave enough to go closer to the witch. It was…a branch with some leaves still on it. It was swaying up and down in the wind. When it rubbed another branch, it squeaked. That was the horrible laugh she heard: "Eeeh!"

It hadn't been a witch, after all.

She said,

"I knew it all along… (etc)"

Sing as before.

She said, "I'm not afraid of anything. But maybe I won't walk in the woods anymore. Maybe I'll walk…in that graveyard."

Do you think that was a good idea? On Halloween night? I don't think so, with the owls and cats and dogs and the wind making such scary sounds. I certainly *hope* you wouldn't do it, but that's what she did.

Audience responds with "yes's" and "no's."

She picked up a stick, went through the gate of the graveyard, and ran her stick along the wrought-iron fence posts: bong, bong, bong, bong.

Audience makes "running a stick" motions and "bong" sound.

Ahead of her, she saw a ghost. It had fiery eyes, and it was looking right at her.

She was so frightened, she was ready to run home, and let her brother tease her, but she remembered her song:

"There's no such thing …(etc)"

Sing; audience sounds.

Even though the sounds around her were scary, the song made her feel brave enough to go closer to the ghost. She could see it. It was…a jack-o'-lantern. Someone had left a carved pumpkin on a tombstone, with a candle in it.

It hadn't been a ghost, after all.

She said,

"I knew it all along…(etc)"

Sing as before.

She said, "I'm not afraid of anything. But maybe I won't walk in the graveyard anymore. Maybe I'll…take this jack-

44

o'-lantern home."

Do you think that was a good idea? On Halloween night? I don't know. I don't think I would have done it. But it's what she did. She picked up the pumpkin and carried it under her arm. The candle was still shining in the jack-o'-lantern.

She went back along the fence: bong, bong, bong, bong.

The light from the pumpkin glistened off the fence posts.

She went back through the woods: crunch, crunch, crunch, crunch.

The light from the pumpkin made shadows move behind the trees.

She went back through the ditch: slurp, slurp, slurp, slurp.

The light from the pumpkin made the vines look deep and sharp.

She went back down the street: step, step, step, step.

As she walked down the street, the flame shone out the jack-o'-lantern's eyes, and made orange reflections in the windows. At last, she came back to her house. But the lights were all out.

Up above, the orange, harvest moon shone down.

The owls hooted.

The cats meowed.

The dogs howled.

The wind wailed around her.

She went up to her door—but there were no sounds in the house, not even her brother teasing anyone.

She turned the doorknob.

She opened the door. It made a loud, squeaky sound.

The only light was the flickering orange flame of her jack-o'-lantern.

She heard a sound under the table. She tried to use the jack-o'-lantern to see what was under there.

When she did, she heard someone breathe in quickly.

	Audience responds with "yes's" and "no's."
	Audience makes "running a stick" motions and "bong" sound.
	Audience makes "walking" motions and "crunch" sound.
	Audience makes "walking" motions and "slurp" sound.
	Audience makes "walking" motions and "step" sound.
	Audience makes sounds as before.
	Audience makes sound.
	Audience makes sound.

She heard a sound behind the couch. She used the jack-o'-lantern to see what was behind there.

When she did, she heard a little yelp. *Audience makes sound.*

She heard a sound in the closet. She used the jack-o'-lantern to see what was in there.

When she did, she heard a shriek. *Audience makes sound.*

She put the jack-o'-lantern on the table, and ran to the light switch and turned it on.

Her Father was hiding under the table.

Her mother was hiding behind the couch.

Her sister was on the floor, with a blanket over her.

Her brother, who always teased her, was hiding in the closet, holding the door shut with both hands.

She said, "What happened?"

Her brother came out of the closet and said, "After you left, we told ghost stories. When we got to the one about the Headless Ghost, we started to get scared. And then we saw a ghost coming down the street with its head under its arm. We knew it was the Terrible Headless Ghost. It came up our walk. It opened our door. It looked at each of us. It put its head on our table. Then it was you."

The little girl said, "Don't you know?

   "There's no such thing...(etc)" *Sing; audience sounds.*

Her mother and father and brother all replied, "We weren't really scared, you see,

   "We knew it along...(etc)" *Repeat, if necessary, to give feeling of satisfying ending.*

NOTES

Using "I Knew It All Along"

The opening song, "I knew it all along," can be a vehicle for discussing fear. Either sing it to the melody given here, or speak it rhythmically, or make up your own melody. Use it for making up movements, or for a story game (see below).

Making up movements game

To use this song for "making up movements," start by singing it. Then say, "What do people do when they get scared?" If the answer is, for example, "They shake all over," then say, "Good. Can you shake as you say this?" Continue asking for more things people do when scared.

Story Game

To use this song for a "story game," start by singing it. Then say, "Did you ever get scared by something, and then find out it wasn't what you thought? Sing it to me, and I'll tell you about a time that happened to me." Sing the song again, then tell an appropriate story:

Once, I was walking across the field by my house, late at night. Then, ahead of me, I saw a ghost. It had long white fingers, and it was waving them at me. I wanted to turn around and run, but something seemed to be making me go closer to it. Then I saw what it was. It was clothing my neighbor had left on his line. I said, "I knew it all along...."

Background on the story

Ellis Parker Butler wrote a story called "Dey Ain't No Ghosts" (©1913, The Century Company), which was printed in the Modern Library anthology, **BEST GHOST STORIES** (Introduction by Arthur B. Reeve, Random House, NY. n.d.). Unfortunately, Butler's language and characterization rely on stereotypes that should prevent it from being reprinted except in documentary histories of racism. A shorter, less offensive version of Butler's story appears in **HALLOWEEN FUN**, edited by Lynn and Katherine Rohrborough (Cooperative Recreation Service, Delaware, OH, n.d. Pages 28-31). It's followed by suggestions for oral telling. Using ideas from these stories, I created "There's No Such Thing." To emphasize the theme of courage, I made up the songs. Jay O'Callahan gave many helpful suggestions to this story. I especially remember his insistence that the brother be "hoist by his own petard."

THERE'S NO SUCH THING

I KNEW IT ALL ALONG

I knew it all a – long____,   I
knew it all a – long____.
Don't you know you can't   fool   me?   I
knew it all a – long____.

This age group achieves the most satisfying balance between enthusiastically jumping on to the wave with the teller and providing a very easy ride.

These stories have a little less active participation, and more active listening. This age group still loves participating, but they may need some extra encouragement from you. A nod of your head will often be enough to give them permission to join in the sounds and actions. The plots and characters are generally more complex, and the themes they explore are more mature, though humor is still an important element in all of the stories.

You will find the familiar participation techniques of song, repetition, action, sound, questions, anticipation, active listening, and weather. In addition the storytellers will be inviting your empathy more directly.

The Ghost's Gold

Introduction

Before you begin the story, rehearse *The Ghost's Song* with an agreed upon signal to join in, such as a beckoning wave of the teller's hand. *The Ghost's Song* is sung with two hands cupped to the singer's mouth as if making a far away call. Before I start the narrative, I like to set the scene by saying, "This story begins in a graveyard. A miserly old Squire has just been buried. . . . "

NARRATIVE

AUDIENCE RESPONSE OR TELLER'S ACTION

No one wept when the old man died. He was a mean old man and no one cried. They buried him in a vault and thanked goodness he was gone...till the night they heard his mournful song...

    "WHOOOOOO! I weep and moan!

WHOOOOOO! If I had only known!

Do your good before you're gone.

When you're dead it's too late,

Do it now.

Don't wait!

WHOOOOOOOOO! It's the ghost's gold!"

Gesture for listeners to join in.

Doors would open and close by themselves. Dishes would fly 'round the room off their shelves! Doors would creak and the shutters would moan. No one dared to sleep alone.

At night the women would feel cold fingers tickling their toes.

Spoken very quietly.

"Tee Hee Hee Hee Hee Hee Hee! It's the ghost's gold!"

Spoken loudly in a wicked, ghostly voice to startle listeners.

"What's the Ghost's Gold?" said the widow to her daughters as they clung to their mother, and each to each other. But no one knew what it was. And night after night this strange sad song kept them awake.

"Perhaps," they thought, "it has something to do with the Squire who was just buried in the vault. He certainly loved gold!"

"But what did he do," asked the mother, "that he cannot rest in peace. Why must he wail and moan? The living cannot help the dead...Be off with your dreadful woe!!"

But wonder as they might, they heard each night,

"It's the Ghost's Gooooooold!"

Sung in a ghostly voice.

When he was alive, the Squire was such a mean and selfish man that he had no friends, except his faithful servant Hans. Hans came to the mistress of the house and offered to visit the dead man in his tomb.

"Perhaps," said Hans, "I will be able to discover why he haunts the household. Build *me* a coffin. I have a plan!"

A coffin was made, and, *alive*, Hans was put in it. Pall bearers carried Hans across the long dark lawn to the family vault in the graveyard. He was laid beside the dead Squire's casket. They left him in that cold eerie place.

Hans lay still for a long time. At the stroke of midnight, he heard the coffin beside him opening!

Listeners may join the storyteller in making a creaking sound of a coffin lid opening.

Hans slowly peeked out. His astonished eyes saw the Squire rise from his death bed, turn to him, and say, "Be you among the living? Or, be you among the dead?"

The storyteller may mime peeking out of the coffin and shudder at being discovered.

"I'm dead," Hans said. "Don't you recognize me? I'm your faithful coachman Hans. I served you in life and I've come to serve you in death as well."

"Then come with me," said the ghost, "I'm bound to disturb the household."

Hans followed the ghost through the graveyard, across the long dark lawn to the house. The ghost floated through the front door. Hans scrambled through an open window.

Hans watched in amazement as the ghost took dishes off the shelves and flung them into the air. The dishes whirled about and crashed onto the floor in ten thousand pieces. Then the ghost waved his hand and the pieces rose up, reassembled themselves and flew back onto the shelves.

The ghost took a dish, handed it to Hans and said, "Here Hans, I want to see you amuse yourself."

Hans took the dish from the ghost and flung it into the air. It whirled about and landed on the floor in ten thousand pieces. Hans waved his hand, just as he had seen the ghost do, but the pieces remained where they were.

The ghost scowled, "Be you among the living? Or, be you among the dead?"

"I'm dead," Hans said. "It's just that I haven't had much practice at haunting. Why do you play at this foolishness?"

The ghost heaved a sigh and said, "I play and sing to ease my sorrow...Woe is me! It's the Ghost's Gold!"

And the ghost began to sing his mournful song...

Teller beckons the listeners to join in.

"WHOOOOOOOOO! I weep and moan!

WHOOOOOOOOO! If I had only known!

Do your good before you're gone.

When you're dead it's too late,

Do it now.

Don't wait!

WHOOOOOOOOO! It's the GHOST'S GOLD!"

"What's the ghost's gold?" asked Hans.

"It's the gold," said the moaning ghost, "that my father gave me on his deathbed. I was supposed to deliver it to the orphanage. But, I KEPT IT! And I kept it a SECRET as well! Now I am DEAD and I cannot tell. The gold cannot do any good in the world, for not a living soul knows that I buried it in the cellar!"

The ghost is very upset,

"Where in the cellar?" asked Hans.

Hans' reply is deadpan.

The ghost led his trusted servant down the dank cellar steps to a moldy corner. As the ghost waved his hand in the air, the ground opened. Up out of the dark hole floated a huge cauldron filled with old gold coins.

Just then, the cock crowed. At the first rays of light, the ghost vanished. The cauldron disappeared, the hole closed, and the ground was as tight as a skin.

Hans rushed upstairs and woke everyone in the household. With sharp shovels they dug in the place Hans pointed. Sure enough, they came upon a rusty cauldron. It was filled with old gold coins.

"We're rich!" the family cried.

But Hans told them they must deliver the gold to the children in the village orphanage.

It was done.

And that night...No ghostly sound was heard. The dishes stayed on the shelves where they had been placed and the ghost did not appear again.

Except once...when Hans was an old man. He told his grandchildren that he was awakened in the night by a voice in his ear.

"Thank you," was all he heard.

NOTES

This story is based on a tale of a legendary Hungarian Squire and his coachman "Janos", or Hans. Heather Forest has adapted it, and added her original song.

THE GHOST'S SONG

Do your good be____ - fore you're gone. When you're dead it's too late. Do it

now, don't wait! WHOOOOOOOOOO! It's the Gho - st's Gold.

The Sprightly Tailor

Introduction

Here's an old tale from Scotland. Your part will be to say with the Tailor;
"I see that, but I'll sew this!"
If you have a roar in you, feel free to be the monster who keeps saying;
"Do you see this____. (I'll fill in the blank.)
Later on, there's a chase, where you can be the sound of running, "Blim blam, blim blam" and "Boom Boom."

NARRATIVE

AUDIENCE RESPONSE
OR TELLER'S ACTION

High on a hill in Scotland, near a castle called Saddell belonging to the great Laird MacDonald, is an old graveyard. The church beside it has nearly rotted away. Its stones are all crumbled and fallen to the ground. It's a peaceful place in the daytime but no one goes near it at night because of the *terrible thing* that's seen there.

"Terrible Thing" is a wonderful phrase to play with vocally.

On nights when the fog swirls over the land, its roars can be heard. On nights when the moon is full, its dark shape is seen like a tree gone mad shaking its fist at the sky.

Down in the valley, below the graveyard, there lived a tailor, called Angus. He was a sprightly man. Quick of eye and finger. Quick of mouth, too. A bit too quick. For once, while lifting an elbow in the tavern, he let fly with, "Aye, I could finish a tartan in the Laird's graveyard before the thing would have time to grab me!" Everyone laughed but some nodded, knowing his skill.

Word came to the Laird of the tailor's boast and he sent for him. The little man stood before the great one who sat sprawled in a chair before the fire with his hounds beside him. "Angus, the tailor, I've heard you boast you could finish a tartan in my graveyard at midnight."

"Aye, I said that." answered Angus.

"Good, you'll get your chance for I'm needing some trews."

The storyteller can explain that "trews are pants and vest sewed together and they're very fine for dancing or walking.

"I'd have you sew them in my graveyard. And every stitch must be finished there, else you'll not get the prize."

The Laird lifted a bag beside him and shook it. Angus' eyes widened for, like many Scots, the clink of coin was music to his ears.

"Are you interested?" asked the Laird.

"Aye, you've a bargain," answered Angus. "How will it be fasted?"

"By my word!" the Laird roared. And Angus left.

That night Angus climbed the hill to the graveyard. The mist was rising from the ground, winding round and round the little man like an old woman's long grey hair. It was quiet. Nothing stirring, yet. Angus stepped carefully around the graves, for some had fallen through and he didn't want to start the night climbing out of rot and mold. He found one gravestone that still stood erect. He'd brought a lantern which he lit and placed beside him. Down in the village, a dog howled at the moon which was half covered by a black cloud. Dark winged things flew overhead. A cold wind blew. Soon the village could not be seen for fog.

Angus had finished the vest and was starting the pants when the ground began to shake. The tombstone he sat on tilted; the lantern slid to the ground and went out. Stones and bones were rising and falling. Something was coming out. It was large dark and round. The size of a boulder. Its eyes were like fire and its mouth full of flames and when the head was clear of the dirt, it roared.

"Do you see this great head of mine!?"

Those of the audience who wish to roar, will be signaled to take the part of the monster.

"Aye, I see that but I'll sew this!!!"

Signal for the rest to say the words "I see that, but I'll sew this" along with the storyteller.

And Angus stitched away.

There was more rumbling and tossing and out came the chest, all full of scales and slime.

"Do you see this great chest of mine?"

Monsters join in.

"Aye, I see that but I'll sew this!!"

Tailors repeat phrase.

And Angus stabbed at the cloth.

There was more thunder and both of its arms burst out of the ground. They were only three feet away and smelled of slime.

"Do you see these great arms of mine?"

Monsters.

"Aye, I see that, and smell it too, but I'll sew this!"

Tailors.

The stitches were getting longer and longer.

The monster was pulling out one of its legs. He stamped it on the ground which shook like judgement day!

"Do you see this great leg of mine?"

Monsters. By this time they should be into it and need little coaching.

"Aye, I see that but I'll sew this!"

Tailors.

Angus knew when the thing pulled the other leg out he would be dead. His stitches were longer and longer and longer. He could see the monster's knee. He made the last stitch, knotted the thread, picked up his lantern and ran!

The monster gave a great roar and the wind that he made sent the tailor on faster. His knees met his chin and the sound that he made as he ran was:

"Blim blam, blim blam, blim blam, blim blam."

Gesture for the audience to join in on the running.

And the monster came!
BOOM BOOM BOOM BOOM

Invite the "Booming" sounds.

And the tailor ran!
"Blim blam, blim blam, blim blam, blim blam."

Audience joins in.

And the monster came!
BOOM BOOM BOOM BOOM

Audience joins in.

"DO YOU SEE ME? DO YOU SEE ME? DO YOU SEE ME?"
roared the monster.

"Yes, yes, yes but I'll do this, this, this!"

They ran down the valley like the stream with a flood on
it.

The tailor reached the castle and just got inside as the
monster REACHED OUT for him.

ROARRRRRRRRRRRR!!!!!!!!!!!!

If you're feeling brave,
you may invite
audience to join the
Roaring.

The monster was so mad at missing his prize, he
slammed his great hand into the wall and THAT print can
be seen there to this day. But day was nigh and he had to
go back to his hole in the ground.

The tailor got his prize and the Laird got his trews. And at
the next dance the Laird did a fancy step and the overlong
stitches all came out. And there was the Laird naked as
the day he was born. The people laughed and thought it
only fair after what he put the tailor through!

And that is the end of this tale!!

NOTES

This story, collected by Joseph Jacobs, was first heard from Cuthbert Bede in the 1800's in
Cantyre, Scotland. A remote relative of my own was part of Clan MacDonald whose
sometimes head was that same Laird of Saddell castle. In this story, though, I favor the
tailor over the Laird.

ADAPTED BY
NANCY SCHIMMEL

Wait Till Martin Comes

Introduction

This is a story with repetitive phrases that an audience may or may not join in on. I start the first "Shall we do it now?" eagerly, and gradually work up to gleeful and sinister for the last one. The answers are all matter-of-fact. This story is good for relief after a genuinely scary one.

NARRATIVE

AUDIENCE RESPONSE OR TELLER'S ACTION

There's a woods up North of here where a man got lost, some time back. He was walking along a wagon track, late in the day, and after a while the wagon track petered out, and it was just a narrow trail. Then it got dark and he lost the trail. He knew he should stop; he was probably just going around in circles, but he was so cold he couldn't bear to stop. So he kept going, getting tireder and tireder. Then he saw a little glow of light, looked like somebody's fire way off in the distance, so he made his way towards it. Got there sooner than he thought he would, 'cause it was just the coals of a fire, inside a cabin, with the door standing wide open. The man went up to the door and said "Hello?" and looked in, but he couldn't see anybody. They must have just stepped out, 'cause the coals were still glowing, and there was a bed all made up.

The man was so tired and cold he just kicked off his shoes and dove into that bed without so much as a by-your-leave. He was getting a little warmed up when a kitten walked in the door, walked three times around the bed, spat in the fire, and sat down on the hearth. The man thought this was pretty strange, and he was lying there puzzling about it when a tom cat walked in the door, walked three times around the bed, spat in the fire, and sat down next to the kitten.

The kitten turned to the tom cat and said, "Shall we do it now?"

"Nope," said the tom cat. "We got to wait till Martin comes."

Well, now that man was scared, and he was thinking he should get out of there, when in through the door walked a bobcat. Bobcat walked three times around the bed, spat in the fire and sat down next to the tom cat. The tom cat and the kitten turned to the bobcat and said, "Shall we do it now?"

Here the storyteller may gesture for the audience to join in the repeated phrase of "Shall we do it now."

"Nope, said the bobcat, "we got to wait till Martin comes."

By now the man wanted to be out of there more than anything, but he was so scared he couldn't move a muscle. And in the door walks a mountain lion. Mountain lion walks three times around the bed, spits in the fire, and sits down next to the bobcat. The bobcat, the tom cat and the kitten all turn to the mountain lion and say, "Shall we do it now?"

Gesture for participation. Lead them in the tone of voice you want. Facial expressions can also help give the signal.

"Nope," says the mountain lion. "We got to wait till Martin comes, and Martin...ain't...coming."

And with that, the mountain lion, the bobcat, the tom cat and the kitten all get up and walk out the door.

And that's the last anyone ever saw of them.

NOTES

I guess I first heard this story at summer camp. It's a popular place for ghost stories. Later I found a version of it in **TALES TO BE TOLD IN THE DARK** by Basil Davenport (Dodd, 1953).

ADAPTED BY

ROBERT E. RUBINSTEIN

Witches On A Mountain

Introduction

This is a story about witches, witches on a mountain. It is fun to tell in a darkened room with a wooden surface nearby for surprise knocking.

You can help divide the audience into halves. One half will be "the witches;" the other half will be "the voice from outside."

Give each half signals so they will know when to start and stop sounds or words. Once the audience has been divided, and the control signals have been taught, you may begin.

NARRATIVE	AUDIENCE RESPONSE OR TELLER'S ACTION
Now, lets hear the witches cackle evilly in high-pitched voices.	Signal half to begin to cackle: "Cackle, Cackle. Heee Heee!"
The witches call out: "Who's knocking at the door ? Whooooo? Whooooo?" and then: "Get along, dooooo! We're cooking for ourselves! Who will cook for youuuuuu?"	Rehearse both refrains with the signal: "The witches called:"
The "Voices" answer: "I'm cold through and throuuuugh - and hungry tooooo! Let me in doooo!"	Rehearse the refrain with the signal: "The voice answered:"
The voices are also the wind blowing, and the knocking.	Have them blow like the wind, and either knock rhythmically on a surface, or say, "Knock, knock."
Don't forget when you're a witch to show your scrunched faces and crooked, curled fingers.	Signal: "Cackle, cackle. Hee - hee!"
When you're the wind, cup your hands around your mouth and purse your lips.	Demonstrate this as well.
And when the witches become owls, don't forget to flap your arms as you fly away.	Demonstrate this as well.

Let's begin.

It was the dark of Halloween Eve. Deep in the forest, in an old, broken-down house, sat three witches cooking their supper.

Outside, the wind howled. The shutters banged and branches beat against the old house.

Signal voices: "Blowing"

Inside the house, the three witches ate and talked of the evil spells they would weave on innocent people when it turned mid-night of Halloween Eve.

Signal: "Cackle, Cackle! Heee - Heee - Heee!"

When out of the forest night, came a knocking.

Either have them say: "Knock, knock," or have them knock rhythmically on some surface.

The witches called:

"Who's knocking at the door? Whoooo? Whoooo?"

The voice answered:

"One who is cold through and throuuuugh - and hungry, toooooo!"

The witches called back:

"Get along doooo. We're cooking for ourselves. Who will cook for you? Whooo? Whooooo?"

The voice said not a word, but the knocking continued.

Either have them knock, or say, "Knocking, Knocking."

Then, the witches called again:

"Who's knocking at the door? Whoooo? Whooo?"

A Voice answered:

"One who is cold through and throuuuugh, and hungry, toooo?"

The witches laughed and cackled.

Laugh and cackle. Then say, "We're cooking for ourselves. Who will cook for you? Whooo? Whooo?"

The Voice said not a word, but the knocking continued: Then, one witch got up from the table. She walked over to the stove, and dropped a piece of dough, the size of a pea, into a frying pan.

Knocking

Witches cackle and laugh.

The dough began to swell and swell. It filled the frying pan and spilled onto the floor. It began to spread out over the floor. The witches screamed

From here on, the Voices keep knocking and knocking. The rhythm of the knocking increases in pace, led by the teller.

Witches scream.

Knocking increases

The voice said not a word, but the knocking continued.

The witches ran for the door but the door was shut tight, and would not open. The witches screamed and cried out again:

Witches scream.

"Who's knocking at the door? Whooo? Whooo?"

The voice said not a word, but the knocking continued.

The dough began to fill the room. The witches climbed up on the stairs. They watched the dough climb up the chairs and then climb up their gnarled limbs. Again they cried out:

"Who's knocking at the door? Whooo? Whooooo?"

Knocking increases in intensity.

The Voice said not a word but the knocking continued.

The eyes of the witches bulged out as they watched the dough swallow their bodies and climb up towards their necks. And they screamed one last time:

"WHO'S KNOCKING AT THE DOOR? WHOOOO? WHOOOOO?"

And the knocking stopped. And the voices called out:

"Fly out the window. Dooooo! There's no more house for youuuuuuu!"

And the conjure-wife witches spread their arms and flew off into the forest night, calling:

Witches spread their arms and flap them like birds.

"Whoooo, whoooooo, whoo will cook for youuuuu?"

And they became the conjure-wife owls.

If you go into the woods at night, you can still hear them calling:

Whoooo, whooooooo, whoo will cook for youuuuu?"

Witches: "Cackle, cackle. Heee, hee..."

But beware! For at midnight on Halloween Eve, they change back into witches weaving their spells.

NOTES

Robert Rubinstein has been telling this story for over twenty years. He first heard it told at various storytelling gatherings, then read a version of it by Frances G. Wickes entitled, "The Conjure Witches," (**GHOSTS AND GOBLINS**, New York: E.P. Dutton & Co., Inc., 1936, rev. 1965.)

The Witch Song

Introduction

I wrote "The Witch Song." for the children of Blue Fairyland, a day care center were I worked in the mid 70's. Having read one too many stories about evil, unkind witches, I decided to set the record straight the best way I knew how -- in song.

Chorus

C · Dm · G · C · C · Dm

Who were the witch-es? Where did they come from? May – be your great – great –

G · C · Dm · G · Am

great – grand – ma was one. Witch – es were wise, wise, wo – men they say, and

C · Dm · G · C

there's a lit – tle witch in ev – ery wo – man to – day_____ .

Verse

Am · G · F

1. Witch – es know all a – bout flow – ers and weeds, how to use all their roots and their

leaves and their seeds. When peo – ple grew wear – y from hard work – in' days, they

made 'em feel bet – ter in so ma – ny ways.

2. When women had babies the witches were there
   To hold them and help them and give them care.
   Witches knew stories of how life began.
   Don't you wish you could be one? Well, maybe you can.

3. Some people thought that the witches were bad.
   Some people were scared of the power they had.
   But power to help and to heal and to care
   Isn't something to fear, it's a pleasure to share.

NOTES

"The Witch Song" can be heard on the Plum City Players' recording, *Plum Pudding* available through Sister's Choice Records, 1450 6th Street, Berkley, CA 94710

ADAPTED FROM THE BROTHERS GRIMM BY
FRAN STALLINGS

The Three Apprentices

The audience, divided in thirds, speaks the peculiar parts of the three apprentices. Rather than rehearse the audience before the story, I prefer to introduce their tasks when the apprentices receive them. Before I start I do mentally decide where I'm going to divide the audience. I begin distinguishing the thirds (I, II, III) with gestures long before they get their parts.

NARRATIVE	AUDIENCE RESPONSE OR TELLER'S ACTION
Once, long ago, there were three very good friends. One was apprenticed to a master butcher, to learn his trade. One was learning to be a baker. And the third was a blacksmith's apprentice.	Point at your Group I = butcher Point at your Group II = baker Point at your Group III = blacksmith
At last the three apprentices were ready to go out on their own. They wanted to stay together, but nowhere could they find a city or town that needed not only a new butcher, but also a new baker, <u>and</u> a new blacksmith! They travelled, looking for work, until they had run out of money -- and hope.	Point at your groups I,II,III as you speak.
"It is clear that we must split up and work in different towns," they decided sadly, "but we will keep in touch. Let's ask the innkeeper in the next town if we can send news to his inn, so that we can always find each other."	
They had just agreed on this plan when a fine carriage came along the road, pulled by fiery black horses whose horseshoes seemed to strike sparks from the pavement. To the amazement of the three apprentices, the carriage stopped beside them and a richly dressed man stepped out.	
From his plumed hat to his polished boot, he looked like a nobleman. But then they saw that he had only ONE boot. The other foot was a hoof. And they knew who he was. That's right. The Evil One: the Devil himself.	Gesture for high hat, down for boot Point at foot. Exchange significant glances

"Good day, young friends," the Devil greeted them. "You seem very unhappy. Perhaps I can help you."

with audience. They may not be familiar with this motif but will catch on.

The three apprentices shrank away from the Evil One. "We want no help from you," they said. "You will try to steal our immortal souls."

Use a low, sly, menacing voice for the Evil One, and lighter, innocent voices for the three apprentices.

The Devil just laughed. "I am after far bigger game. There is someone in the next town who is half mine already! I need just a little help to capture his soul. If you do as I say, I will give you so much money that you can live like fine gentlemen. You will never have to work."

Indicate doubt, amazement.

The apprentices looked at each other. If they didn't need to find three jobs, they could stay together. "But what do you want us to do?" they asked. "We won't do anything bad or cruel."

The Devil smiled. "You must agree to speak *only* when someone asks you a question. You may say *only* the words I tell you, and always *in this order*.

Emphasize these instructions heavily.

The first one," he pointed to the butcher's apprentice, "must always say, 'All three of us'".

Point to your Group I.

"The second," he pointed to the baker's apprentice, "must say, 'Money.'"

Point to your Group II.

"And the third," the blacksmith's apprentice, "can only say, 'That's right'. Will you do it?"

Point to your Group III.

The three apprentices talked it over. Those words were not evil or nasty -- were they? By saying those words they couldn't hurt anyone or get into trouble -- could they? Right. If there was a trick in it, they couldn't find it. It seemed completely harmless, and the reward was great!

Direct this question to the audience.

Again. A few may answer aloud; many will shake their heads, "No".

Shrug: no problem here!

"Very well," they said, "we agree."

The Devil smiled. "Here is a wallet. Whenever you need money, take all you need. It will always be full. And I want you to stay at the finest inn in the city. The finest one, no other. Do you understand?" The three apprentices gladly agreed. "And remember," said the Evil One, "you may say no words except the ones I have given you, and you must always speak in that order." They agreed.

They can't get in any trouble that way, can they? Let's try it. This third of the audience: you speak for the first apprentice, the butcher. All you can say is, "All three of us." Try it.

Again, loud and clear --

Good!

And you in the middle: you speak for the second apprentice, the baker. What was his line?

I <u>know</u> you can say that. Louder!

Good!

Now you folks over here: you speak for the third apprentice. All he could say was, "That's right!"

Again, louder!

Good. Now we can see how it worked out.

When the three apprentices arrived at the inn, ragged and dirty from their travels, the innkeeper did <u>not</u> welcome them. "Go away, you vagabonds! Do you think you can stay here?" he demanded.

The butcher's apprentice said, --

"And how do you expect to pay," he asked.

The baker's apprentice replied, --

"Oh, really? You ragged beggars have money?"

The blacksmith's apprentice said, --

"Well, in that case..." The innkeeper invited them in. "Dinner will soon be served," he added. "Will you, ah... dine here?"

The butcher's apprentice said, --

"My meals are not cheap," the innkeeper warned.

The baker's apprentice said, --

"Well, if you feel like spending it," the innkeeper agreed.

The third apprentice added --

After dinner, the three apprentices went up to their room. A maid came to ask who wanted a bath.

Now address the audience directly.
Point to I.
I: "All three of us."
I: "ALL THREE OF US!"

Point to II
II: "Money"
II: ""MONEY!"

Point to III.
III: "That's right!"
III: "THAT'S RIGHT!"

I: "All three of us."

II: "Money".

III: "That's right!"

I: "All three of us."

II: "Money".

III: "That's right!"
The audience is pleased that these three replies prove adequate to the situation. They are not making fools of themselves. Yet.

The butcher's apprentice said, --

"All three *at once?*" she stared. "Very well, sirs, I'll bring you some soap."

The baker's apprentice said, --

"Money? You use money instead of soap? Why, that will make you dirtier than you are already!"

-- said the third.

She ran downstairs and told the servants about the strange young men. The other guests also began to think the three apprentices were odd. When someone asked where they had come from,

the first apprentice had to reply, --

A little puzzled, the guest kept asking. "Oh, you all came from the same town? What is its name?"

"Really! I never heard of that town. It must be quite far away."

And that's what happened whenever people tried to talk with them. For instance, when somebody sneezed, a guest said, "Gesundheit! Have you got a cold?"

"What a shame, all three at once. What medicine have you tried?"

"Gracious, that's an odd medicine."

The three apprentices used the never-empty wallet to buy fine clothes. They had good food and comfortable lodgings. But they soon realized that everyone thought they were crazy. Nobody trusted them! But at least they were still together.

One night, however, a rich merchant stopped at the inn and came secretly to the innkeeper. "Good sir," he said, "I am worried about my safety. I have a great treasure with me. My room is next to those three crazy apprentices, and I'm afraid they will try to rob me in the night."

This suggested an evil plan to the greedy innkeeper. Several times in past years he had quietly robbed and murdered a rich guest, burying the body in his cellar and telling everyone that the man had to leave in the night. But people were just a bit suspicious. Now, he realized, he could do it again and pin the blame on these three crazy apprentices. No one would suspect him.

I: "All three of us."

II: "Money."

III: "That's right --"

I: "All three of us."

II: "Money."

III: "That's right."

I: "All three of us."

II: "Money."
III: "That's right."

Take the audience into your confidence here, letting them in on the evil plan.

70

In the middle of the night, he crept down the hall and murdered the merchant: not carefully and bloodlessly,as he had always done before, but with an axe! He hid the merchant's chest of gold in the cellar with the rest of his stolen treasure. But he left the body lying in its blood.

In the morning, when the maid went in to bring the merchant his tea, she shrieked in terror at the bloody sight! Everyone came running. The innkeeper pretended to be surprised and horrified. "Who can have done this terrible deed?" he asked, looking right at the apprentices.

The poor butcher's apprentice could only reply --

"How terrible!" exclaimed a guest. "Why did you do it?"

The second apprentice could only say --

"Then you admit that you did it?" demanded the innkeeper. And the third had to say --

In an appalled voice.

I: "All three of us."

II:"Money."

III:"That's right."
Forced to incriminate themselves, the audience starts to get uneasy.

The police took the three apprentices off to jail and the innkeeper thought he was getting away scot free. At the trial, the judge asked, "Which one of you planned this crime?"

"And what was your motive?"

"Then I pronounce you guilty of murder."

I: "All three of us."
II: "Money."
III: "That's right."
They are even more uncomfortable; voices often fail here although they know their parts perfectly well.

The judge sentenced them to be hung at dawn the next morning. You can imagine that they could not sleep, sadly regretting the day they had agreed to say such "harmless" words for the Devil.

The next morning they were led out to the gallows. All the townsfolk had gathered to watch the hanging , including the innkeeper. Suddenly, a fine carriage came thundering into town. Sparks flew from the hoofs of the horses as they galloped over the cobblestones; lightning seemed to dart from their eyes. The carriage pulled to a stop at the gallows and a richly dressed nobleman stepped out. You know who he was…

Significant glance to audience.

"My lords," he addressed the judge and lawyers, "we would not want innocent people to be hanged while the guilty man goes free! My three young friends, on the night of the murder, did you hear a noise in the hallway outside your room?" The butcher's apprentice replied nervously --

I: "All three of us."
Audience is nervous too.

"Did you hear a metallic clink, like the sound of something in a box?"

The baker's apprentice said --

II: "Money."

"Oho! So you heard the merchant's treasure being taken from his room! But you young fellows did not steal that treasure, did you?"

The blacksmith's apprentice said --

III: "That's right."
They are very relieved that this will turn out all right after all.

"Now," said the Evil One, stepping into the crowd and grabbing the guilty innkeeper by the arm, "can one of you identify this man for me?"

I: "All three of us."

"Of course you know him. He's the innkeeper, who charged you a lot of..."

II: "Money."

"But he took more than that from the unfortunate merchant."

III: "That's right!"

The Devil gave the innkeeper to the police. "Hold this man while someone goes to check in his cellar. There I believe you will find the remains of many wealthy guests this man has quietly murdered, and the treasure he stole from them. But we would never have known of his crimes, if it hadn't been for these young men whom he tried to blame."

Devil inadvertently points at the first apprentice. I: "All three of us."

-- said the first apprentice. "That's all right," whispered the Devil, "your job is done now. You can say anything you wish."

"Hooray," they shouted, "that was almost too close for comfort!"

The police found the bones and treasure in the innkeeper's cellar, as the Devil had promised. So the innkeeper hung on the gallows prepared for the three apprentices. And the Devil got the innkeeper's evil soul for his ... collection.

"Thank you for your help," he told the three apprentices. "I was tired of waiting for that one. You did your part well. You may keep the never-empty wallet, and may you enjoy a long life of leisure." And as far as I know, they did. But they were very careful *never again* to say --

(<u>Finale</u>: point to all three in sequence)

I: "ALL THREE OF US!"

II: "MONEY!"

III: "THAT'S RIGHT!"

NOTES

This story is freely and extensively adapted from a short tale which appears as #120 in <u>The Complete Grimm's Fairy Tales</u> (Pantheon paperback, © 1944, 1972, pp 542-545). Trial and error with many different audiences led to the present version for contemporary listeners. In the Bible Belt I sometimes have to avoid saying "Devil", although oddly enough I can often get away with "Evil One".

The original tale gives only a few examples of how the three apprentices used their limited speech in appropriate -- and absurd -- ways. I have added more, some suggested by listeners. Let the audience's patience and enjoyment guide you on how many examples to include. High school and adult audiences have enjoyed this additional scene:

The waitress in the dining room thought the three apprentices were very attractive. One evening as she cleared their table she whispered, "Would one of you handsome fellows like to go walking with me in the moonlight tonight?" The butcher's apprentice replied enthusiastically --

I: "All three of us!"

"All three! Well, I don't know..." --

II: "Money."

"Heavens! I'm <u>not</u> that kind of girl!" She flounced away angrily.

The blacksmith's apprentice sadly said, --

III: "That's right."

My ending differs from the original one where the Devil simply commands, "You three are innocent; you may now speak, make known what you have seen and heard." My husband suggested that it would be more satisfying if the same words which got them <u>into</u> trouble could also get them <u>out</u> again. Audiences seem relieved and appreciative!

In some subcultures it is very impolite to point. Designate your three groups by holding up the following hand signs, and nodding toward the group. I ("All three of us") = hold up first three fingers; II ("Money") = rub fingers against thumb; III ("That's right") = index finger and thumb together, other fingers fanned. (NB: This sign is obscene in other cultures.)

Follow-up Activities

1. The "Devil" turns up in many of the tales which Jacob and Wilhelm Grimm collected. Read some of these stories (a few are #29 The Devil with the Three Golden Hairs, #44 Godfather Death, #82 Gambling Hansel, #100 The Devil's Sooty Brother, #125 The Devil and His Grandmother, #195 The Grave Mound) and discuss the Devil's various roles as a stock villain, dupe, or unwitting helper. Compare/contrast with Devil tales from other cultures.

2. The apprentices' limited words sometimes fit the situation, but more often came out sounding absurd depending on the context. Try inventing additional scenes for them, both reasonable and silly.

3. This kind of verbal misunderstanding is a staple of folk humor. "The Squire's Bride" (a Norwegian folktale found in many collections) and "Soap, Soap, Soap" (Richard Chase, **GRANDFATHER TALES**) use it; the Three Stooges' "Who's On First" routine is a classic example. Listen to these. Think of other examples.

4. Try composing such a scene for a story of your own. For example, using all the different meanings/puns for the words "Right" and "Left", devise dialog which first uses those two words as sensible answers, and then makes nonsense with them.

Related Tales

Some Grimms translations call this story (Aarne-Thompson tale type 360) "The Three Journeymen" (another word for "apprentices"). Another version is "The Three Travelling Artisans" (Ranke, Kurt, ed. Folktales of Germany, tr. Lotte Baumann. Folktales of the World. Chicago: University of Chicago Press, 1966. #28.)

Other Devil tales: Stith Thompson's motif index lists a huge number of tales concerning the devil (motif G303-G303.25.18, pp 312-345 in Vol 3).

Uncle Bill's Dream

Introduction

There are still some old-timers who live close enough to the land to know some of the things that happen in the night, in the mountains, in the moonlight. One of them was an old fellow named Uncle Bill Hatfield. And I'll tell you his story as he might have told it himself. There's some witchy words in this story. You can say 'em with me it you'r a mind to.

NARRATIVE

AUDIENCE RESPONSE OR TELLER'S ACTION

Well, I'm not a superstitious man, but there's some things that a lot of folks call superstitions, which is just as true as anything you see in the daylight. Now, you take witches, for instance. No use telling me there ain't none. Why, I've been rode by 'em plenty of times.

One night, my wife and I were asleep in our bed in our cabin up along Little Pine Creek. In my dream, I heard somebody calling my name, so I sat up and looked out the window. And there, in the front yard, was the prettiest looking girl I ever seen. She was motioning for me to come out and join her. Well, I didn't waste my time -- I didn't even put on my shoes. I just walked out there in my white nightshirt. And there, in the moonlight, I could see she was wearing spurs on her boots.

And she had a brand-new bridle in her hand. She reaches out, grabs me by the forelock and shouts out, "Mixti-moxti".

The storyteller can encourage the listeners to join in on "mixti-moxti" with a gesture.

Next thing I know, I'm standing there on four legs with a tail, long ears. Darned if she hadn't turned me into a donkey! Well, before I could even say, "Hee-haw", she slaps that bridle into my mouth, leaps on my back and digs them spurs into my side.

75

Well, I didn't need any more encouragement. I took off like a house afire and she rode me hard for several miles. And it wasn't no easy trail, either. She took me down hills, across streams, through briar patches and thorns. Finally we comes into a clearing, and we met up with a dozen little fellas. They were -- I don't know -- maybe about three feet tall, each one of them carrying a sack just overflowing with gold coins.

Now, I figured maybe they was bank robbers. That Witchy-woman, she climbed down and darned if they didn't load them heavy bags of gold right on my back! Well, they led me up into the trees 'til we come to a cave underneath a cliff and that Witchy-woman tied me up to a white oak sapling, about as big around as a -- I don't know -- about as big around as a woman's ankle. They unloaded them bags and stowed them in the cave.

Well, that Witchy-woman hops on my back, rode me like a brush fire back to the front yard, turns me into a human and sends me to bed. Well, when I woke up the next morning, I was feeling pretty low. I was briar scratched all over, and my arm and leg muscles were sore from running all night. I told my wife what happened and she was sure I'd just been out sleep-walking, so she laughed and she doctored my cuts. But darned if I didn't have that same dream the next night and for five more nights after it. And, each morning, I woke up just lacerated and tired out. My wife, she tried to help me. She tried to loop a piece of rope around my wrist and tie me down to the bedpost, but it didn't do no good. My dream body just went off and got all scratched up just the same.

Then I got an idea. I thought, "maybe I'm having this dream for a reason. Maybe it's because I was meant to go out there and find that cave in the daylight and get that gold." So, on the seventh night, I hatched myself a plan. I laid down in my bed and I fell asleep and waited for that Witchy-woman. Well, there she was, a callin' my name.

I joined her out in the front yard, she grabs me, yells out, "Mixti-moxti".

Gesture for listeners to join in again.

Next thing I know, we're tearing down that trail. But this time, I'm smart. I stops every now and then. I raises my donkey tail and lets drop a little dropping, just to mark the spot. I knew, next day, all I'd have to do is go out there and follow them droppings right up to the cave.

Well, we met up with them little men like we always did before, and they got me loaded and got me up there, and she tied me up to that sapling. All the while, I'm just grinning like a donkey. And then, you know, donkeys -- they have pretty good teeth. I looked down there. I seen that sapling. I decided I was going to mark that spot extra well. And I reached down and I just started to gnaw away at the bark. I was just gnawing and chewing and chewing hard as I could. And then all at once, I hear my wife! I hear her yelling!

I thought: "What's she doing in this dream?" Next thing I know I wake up and there I am, sitting up in bed, chewing on my wife's leg! And not only that, I had made a terrible mess of those bed sheets!

NOTES

This story is a traditional tale which has also been recorded in **BOTKIN'S TREASURY OF AMERICAN FOLKLORE**, by Andrew Botkin (New York: Crown Publishers, 1950.) Robin has included it on his tape, *When the Moon is Full*: Supernatural Stories from the Pennsylvania Mountains," published by Groundhog Press, P.O. Box 181, Springhouse, PA. 19477.

It is simply true that the older we get, the more difficult it is to persuade us to take the risk of jumping on to that wave. However, once we are on it, the ride is deep, imaginative and supremely satisfying.

The stories in this section primarily employ the techniques of empathy and active listening, though repetition of phrase and use of sounds is occasionally found as well. These are a particular type of ghost story that is called an *urban legend*. This is my favorite of all the ghost story types. An *urban legend* is a story that is still alive in the oral tradition. It is told with the belief that it is true. It is always told as if it happened to "a friend of a friend," or a FOAF, but it can never be traced directly to its original source. The *urban legend* uses more detail than any other story type, with the purpose of grounding the listener in the reality of the story. Through this element of belief, the listener is drawn into extremely active listening, creating its strongest participatory element.

After one *urban legend* has been told, it is common for someone in the audience to raise their hand, eager to tell their version of the same story, or to share an *urban legend* of their own. Not only do *urban legends* draw us into mesmerized involvement with the story, they address our deepest fears and concerns. The fear is always revealed in the final seconds of the story with a surprise ending that usually leaves the audience gasping for breath.

The Woman in Grey

Introduction

As with most urban legends, the participation in this story is signaled in the following introductory phrase: "This story comes from Alabama. Whether it's true or not, well that's up to you to decide. But the folks from Alabama where this story takes place, they say it's so."

NARRATIVE	AUDIENCE RESPONSE OR TELLER'S ACTION

One hot day in summer a shopkeeper was working in his shop. Business had been slow and there were no people in the shop now. He decided to go behind the counter and work on his account books. With his head bent low over the books, he sensed that someone had walked in. He looked up. In the doorway stood a tall, thin woman, dressed in grey. "Grey as shadows," the shopkeeper thought to himself. She had a sad, tragic face. Her big, dark eyes were full of tears. She moved slowly to the counter. The shopkeeper stood up, looked at her kindly and said, "What can I do for you today, ma'am?"

Without speaking the woman pointed to a bottle of milk. The shopkeeper took it down and handed it to her. She took the milk, turned around, and went out, without paying or speaking.

The shopkeeper was so touched by her great, sad eyes that he didn't have the heart to go after her and demand payment.

The next day business was slow again. While dusting some of the shelves, the shopkeeper sensed that she had come in the store. He turned around. She was standing in the doorway with the same grey dress and the same great, sad eyes.

He went behind the counter and asked, "What can I do for you today, ma'am?"

Just as before, she pointed to a bottle of milk. He lifted it down and he handed it to her. She took it, turned around, and left the store.

That night he met with some friends to play cards. As he was dealing out the cards, he told his friends about the woman in grey. "She has a secret. I don't know what it is but I'd like to know."

The friends listened to the story and said amongst themselves, "What do you say we come to the shop tomorrow, pretend that we're shopping and if she comes in again, we'll follow her? We'll see what her secret is." It was agreed.

The next day, at about the same time, the shopkeeper was working and his friends were all stationed around as though they were shopping. Within a few minutes, the woman in grey was standing in the doorway. She moved up to the counter.

"What can I do for you today, ma'am?"

Just as before, she pointed to a bottle of milk. He handed it to her. She turned around and went out.

The storekeeper closed his shop. The friends gathered together at the doorway. They were going to hang back so she wouldn't know that she was being followed. They didn't need to worry about that. The woman was moving down the main street so fast, they could barely keep her in sight. Moving right out the end of town and down a country lane, she went on and on until she reached the cemetery. Then she wove in and out amongst the tombstones as though she knew *exactly* where she was going.

After a time she reached a rise in the hill, stood there a moment silhouetted against the sky, then disappeared. The friends came as fast as they could to the spot where she had disappeared. On that spot was a new grave. The grass hadn't even begun to grow over the fresh turned earth. On the tombstone it said that buried there, just four days ago, was a young mother and her infant child. Both had died of a fever.

The friends were standing around, trying to figure out what it was they had seen, when they heard a sound coming from in the grave. It was a long, mournful baby's wail. One of the men ran for a shovel and began to dig.

After a time they exposed the pine casket. The storekeeper reached down and opened it up.

Inside was the woman in grey. She was dead, many days dead. But her baby was alive. It had been in a coma when the mother died and was thought to be dead as well. They had buried that baby alive. The storekeeper picked up the baby and he saw something that made his blood run cold. There, in that grave, were three empty milk bottles.

After that, they covered the grave over and found a home for the baby. The folks down in that Alabama town never saw the woman in grey again. They say it's because now she knows her baby is safe.

NOTES

"The Woman in Grey" first appeared in Sheila Dailey's publication, *Storytelling: A Creative Teaching Strategy*. The first version that Sheila saw was in Maria Leach's **THE THING AT THE FOOT OF THE BED**. She has since come across several variants --"The Woman in White," and another in the oral tradition with no title from the upper peninsula in Michigan. Much of the characterization is Sheila's own elaboration on the story.

Sheila specializes in Great Lakes stories and legends. She believes that in every good ghost story there is an unmet need which the ghost comes back to satisfy. That's what she looks for in a ghost story, the resolution that brings healing to the listeners as well as the characters.

ADAPTED BY
RAFE MARTIN

The Boy Who Drew Cats

Introduction

There are many chances for participation in this story. Sounds, such as the "Boom, boom boom" can be taught before hand, or introduced during the course of the story. You may want to begin by teaching your audience to exclaim, "WHO'S DRAWING CATS AROUND HERE?"

NARRATIVE	AUDIENCE RESPONSE OR TELLER'S ACTION

Once, long ago in Japan, there was a boy who loved to draw cats. This boy lived with his mother and father, and his older brother and sister, on a small farm. One day the earth dried up and the crops withered. No matter how hard this family worked, they could not grow enough for all to eat. It was a time of famine.

Every night the mother and father sat up late worrying about their children. "How will we survive? The older boy and girl are both strong and hard-working. But our youngest is so sensitive and delicate. He might die. What can we do?"

Finally, they decided they would take their youngest son to a nearby temple and leave him there with the monks and priests. Though they might never see him again, at least he would have food.

They told the head priest at the Temple, "We have brought you our son. He is bright and quick. Please let him live here with you, or he will never survive the famine."

The priest agreed and the boy waved goodbye to his parents. They walked down the road getting smaller and smaller -- and then they were gone.

The head of the Temple spoke to the boy, "You are a bright fellow. Everything will work out fine for you here. But we do have one rule. You just don't do what you want to do. Here you do the necessary job, the job you are assigned. Do you understand?"

The boy said that he did.

"Good," said the head of the Temple. "It's late. Go find a place to sleep in the sleeping hall. Tomorrow we shall start you at a useful job."

The boy found a place to sleep on the thick straw-matting of the sleeping hall floor. He unrolled his blanket and took from the loosened bedroll his three precious things: his brush, inkstick, and grinding stone. He put his three precious drawing implements beside him and, feeling comforted in the darkened hall, he fell asleep.

In the morning he got up and did his assigned job along with the others and everything was fine.

The second day he got up and again, did his assigned job along with the others. All went well.

The third day the monks and priests in that temple awoke, stretched and yaaaaawwwwned.

Stretches and yawns, especially if repeated, are great participation opportunities.

They put on their robes and went out into the central hall of the temple and -- WHAT WAS THAT!!! There were cats drawn all over the floors!

"WHO'S DRAWING CATS AROUND HERE?!" they exclaimed.

Let your listeners know that it is time to join in.

Naturally they watched the boy carefully. But they could see nothing out of the ordinary. They let it go by.

The second day after that the monks and priests in that temple awoke, yaaaawwwned and stretched.

More yawning and stretching.

Then they put on their robes and went out into the central hall of the temple and -- WHAT WAS THAT!!!! There were cats drawn on the walls!!!.

"WHO'S DRAWING CATS AROUND HERE?!" they cried again.

Gesture to join in.

And once more they watched the boy carefully. But again, they saw nothing out of the ordinary, and so they let it go by.

The third day came. Once again the monks and priests in that temple got up, yaaaaaawwwwwwned and stretcccchhhhed, put on their robes, went out into the central hall of the temple and looked at the floors.

One more time with the yawning and stretching, and everyone should be very awake and relaxed.

The floors were all right. They looked at the walls. The walls were all right. They looked at the ceilings and the ceilings too were all right. "Whatever it is, it's over," they said in relief. Then they took out their books, opened them to read, and WHAT WAS THAT???!!!!! There were cats drawn in every book!!

They closed their books, put the books away, went to the head of the temple and said, "This new boy is drawing cats all over everything. You must get rid of him. We don't want cats all over everything!"

The head of the Temple called the boy to him. "Are you the one who's drawing cats all over everything?" he asked.

"Yes," admitted the boy slowly, "I don't mean harm by it. I don't mean to destroy temple property or ruin walls or floors or books. It's just that I see a clear stretch of floor or wall, a clear page in a book and I just SEE cats. Please understand."

"Hmm," said the priest. "I understand. You may be an artist. There is certainly an unseen destiny calling you. You must leave here. However, let me give you one piece of advice before you leave. Avoid large places," he said. "Stay in small places."

"Thank you," said the boy, "I will." Then, rolling up his drawing things in his bed roll, he tied the cord around his bundle, threw it over his shoulder, and set out on the road alone.

It was late in the fall. The sky was low and grey. The air was chill and the wind moaned among the trees making the dead leaves rattle on the bare branches like bones -- chhkkuh, chhkkuh, chhkkuh.

Invite the audience to rub their hands or use their voices to make the sounds of the dead leaves.

As the boy walked he grew frightened. Where would he stay? Who would care for him? How would he eat? How would he live? He would starve or freeze!

Then he remembered. About twelve miles away on a hill was a big temple. Perhaps they might be big enough to need an artist. Then he could draw his cats without bothering anyone.

With this hope in his heart he set off for the temple.

What he didn't know was that this temple had been abandoned during the famine. A goblin lived there now.

As the boy walked toward the temple it got darker and colder. At last, just before nightfall, he came to the great entrance gate of the temple. He walked up to the big wooden doors and knocked.

BOOM. BOOM. BOOM.

Another sound your audience could enjoy making with you.

His knocks echoed hollowly. But there was no answer.

"That's funny," he thought, "someone should be here to open the door for travellers. It is the proper way. Ah, it must be because of the famine. They must all still be out working in the fields. Still it is so dark and cold. And I am so hungry and tired I'd better just go inside and wait."

He pushed on the door, Creeeeaaaak!

The creaking of doors is a classic participation opportunity.

"What rusty hinges!" he exclaimed. "Someone should have the job of polishing the hinges. Well, I can do this job. When they return they will give me a home. But it is so dark and cold and I am so tired. I'd better get inside. He pushed the door open, Creeeaaak! and stepped inside.

Again.

There were cobwebs hung along the entrance. "Why they must all be so busy working in the fields," he thought, "they cannot even do these necessary jobs. I'll clean up and when they return they'll give me a home."

He found an old broom and swept up a big area around the entranceway. It was dusty, but, after a while, the job was done.

The temple was silent. The moon was high in the sky and still no one had returned. The boy knew it must be late. The strangeness of it began to bother him. After all, where could they be?

At last he grew so tired he could wait no longer. He untied the cord on his bedroll, unrolled the blanket, and put his three precious things -- brush, inkstick, and grinding stone -- beside him. Then he covered himself over so that he might drift off to sleep. Then he noticed, in the darkness nearby, something white and glimmering. What could it be? He reached out and touched a set of Japanese folding screens -- three frames of wood, hinged together in panels and covered over with rice paper. The boy took a look at those screens and one thought came to his mind.

"CATS!"

The sharp ones in the audience will be eager to say this with you.

In great excitement he ran to the front door and opened it. There in the moonlight a little stream flowed like silver among the dead leaves. He rushed to the stream, scooped up a palmful of the cold water, took it inside, and poured it on his grinding stone. Then he ground up his ink, dipped in his brush, and drew running cats, sitting cats, dancing cats, playing cats, leaping fighting cats, sleeping cats, eating cats, MEOWING CATS, all over the screens.

He stepped back, looked and exclaimed, "At last! My cats have come out perfectly. They are just as I've always hoped they would be. My cats are here at last!"

Washing out his brush and placing his drawing things again beside him, he lay down and, gazing in joy at the painted screens, prepared for sleep.

Suddenly, the priest's parting words came to his mind, "Avoid large places. Stay in small places."

The boy looked around and realized that he was in a big, huge room, the *very kind of room he had been warned against*.

"I've got to find a small place," he said. "Or something terrible will happen. I know it." He looked and looked, and then, behind the screens he saw a small cupboard with a sliding paper door. "That's a small place. I'll go in there." Gathering his drawing things and blanket he crept into that small place, slid the door closed behind him, and at last fell fast asleep.

SUDDENLY! In the middle of the night! There was a horrible howling! There were terrible bloodcurdling noises! Walls were smashed and furniture was broken. Then, just as suddenly, silence. Not a sound.

All night long the little boy lay in that cupboard shaking and shaking, afraid of what was waiting just outside that thin paper door.

In the morning, the moon went down and the sun came up. The sun's light filtered through the walls of the temple. It filtered through the paper door of the little cupboard and the boy knew it was now or never. Either he opened the door and faced what was there, or he might never have the courage to open it again.

He took his blanket and drawing things in one hand and put his other hand on the door of the cupboard. Slowly he slid the door back, just a bit, and peered out. He couldn't see a thing. He was behind the screens.

He slid the door back all the way, gripped his blanket and drawing things firmly in his hand, crept out on the floor, crept along the screens, took a deep breath, and stuck his head around the screens.

There, in the center of that huge room, lay an immense rat-goblin. Dead.

"Oh!" exclaimed the boy, "Who saved me from this horrible monster?"

Then he looked at the screens where he had drawn the cats with so much love and care. From every tooth and claw blood was dripping down the screens. You see, the cats had come to life in the night. It was those cats who saved the boy.

After this, as mysteriously as it had begun, the famine now quickly faded away. By spring every field was bright and green with growing rice. Perhaps the little boy's cats, in destroying the goblin, saved them all. In any case, the famine never came again.

The little boy, safe with his family once more, became a very great artist known throughout the islands of Japan. And, it's said that no matter how great he became, everyday he took out his inkstick and his grinding stone, ground up his ink, poured in the water, dipped in his brush and drew at least one, CAT!

Many will want to join you for this last word.

NOTES

"The Boy Who Drew Cats" is an old Japanese tale. It was first translated into English by Lafcadio Hearn around the turn of the century. Hearn, a newspaper writer of Greek-Irish descent, went to Japan, settled there, married a Japanese woman, and became one of the early communicators of Japanese culture -- which he deeply loved -- to the West.

This version of the tale is based on many years of my own exposure to things Japanese and to many years of performing the story. It was one of the first stories in my repertoire and a story I still love telling today. My telling of "The Boy Who Drew Cats" is recorded on *Ghostly Tales of Japan* (Yellow Moon Press).

The Vampire Skeleton

Introduction

Storyteller: In the old days, these stories were always told in the winter time, usually at night around the fire. It is easy to fall asleep around a fire and, since a story cannot be properly told unless everyone is listening and "part of the story," the storyteller had a special way of seeing if everyone was awake. Occasionally the storyteller would say **HO?** and everyone had to answer back **HEY!** to show they were still "part of the story." As I tell this story, you must do the same.
Storyteller: **HO?**
Audience: **HEY!**
Storyteller: **HO?**
Audience: **HEY!**

NARRATIVE	AUDIENCE RESPONSE OR TELLER'S ACTION
Long ago, a woman was traveling late at night through the forest towards the village of her sister. The full moon shone down brightly and so it was not too dark to travel, though clouds crossing the sky sometimes passed over the face of the moon.	Hold up left hand, palm forward, to indicate the moon, slowly bring your right hand, palm facing you, in front of it to indicate the clouds. Follow this by dropping both hands in a slow sweeping gesture.

Then everything became as dark as the heart of a deep cave and all that could be done was to stand and wait for the clouds to clear away.
Storyteller: **HO?**

Audience: **HEY!**

With this woman was her husband and her small baby. She carried the baby in its cradleboard and on her back she carried bags made of woven bark which were filled with corn. There was a shortage of food in her sister's village, so she was bringing this corn to share with them.

She had hoped to reach her sister's village before dark, but her husband had walked so slowly, that the night had overtaken them. Her husband carried nothing. However, he was a lazy man, and as they walked through the darkness, he complained.

"Why must we travel so far? Why must we take food to your sister's people? We have barely enough food ourselves. My feet hurt from all this walking. I am tired. We need to find a place to rest for the night."

So the husband spoke, but the wife said nothing. She only continued to lead the way, carrying the heavy sacks of corn and her baby in the cradleboard.

Storyteller: **HO?**

Audience: **HEY!**

As they walked along, the path in the forest rose until they were standing on a small hill. Below them was a clearing and the full moon shone brightly down into that clearing, illuminating a small lodge at its northern edge. Just at that moment, the baby started to cry. The husband paid no attention to the baby.

"Ah-huh," he said, "that looks like a good place for us to spend the night."

"My husband," said the wife, "I do not like the looks of that place. Let us continue on to my sister's village. It is not far."

But the husband did not listen. He was already going down the hill. The wife quieted their baby and followed.

Storyteller: **HO?**

Audience: **HEY!**

"Hah!" said the husband, looking inside the open door of the small lodge, which was made of bent saplings with elm bark shingles. "This is a fine place to spend the night."

He went in and the wife followed, holding her baby close. She looked around. The moon shining in made it bright enough for her to see inside the lodge. On one side there was a sleeping rack made of saplings tied together with an old bear skin on top. To the other side of the lodge was a large box, of the sort that people used to store their possessions. The lid of the box was shut.

That was all there was in the lodge, but as she stood there, the woman thought she could feel someone or something watching her.

"My husband," she said, "this is not a good place. Let us continue to my sister's village."

The husband did not listen. "Ah," he said, feeling the bed. "I must get my rest so that I can be strong enough to care for you and your child. I shall sleep here on the bed. You and the child can sleep there on the floor." With that, he lay down and pulled the bear skin over him.

Storyteller: **HO?**

Audience: **HEY!**

The wife was not happy. "My husband," she said, "listen to me." But the husband did not answer. He only snored.

The wife looked around once more and then lay on the floor so that she could see the bright face of Grandmother Moon shining in through the open door. She held her baby close to cover the face of the moon and then . . . allllll wassssss darkkkk.

> The last sentence of this paragraph should be said very slowly, accompanied by the same gesture of left hand held up, palm forward and the other brought across to cover it.

The wife heard something. It was a sound like this.

> Make a creaking sound, like the lid of a box opening.

"My husband," she said, "do you hear that sound?" But the husband did not answer. He only snored.

Storyteller: **HO?**

Audience: **HEY!**

> This call and response should be said very softly.

The wife held her breath and listened. Now she heard another sound, a sound that seemed to be passing . . . slowly . . . by . . . her!

> Make a scratching sound or a clicking sound, like the sound of fingernails scraping on wood or the sound of two pencils tapped together. Experiment with this to find the sound that suits you. You may want to keep two small sticks handy in your pocket to use during this story.

"My husband," the wife whispered, "do you hear that?" But the husband did not answer. He only snored.

Storyteller: **HO?**

Spoken softly.

Audience: **HEY!**

Again the wife held her breath and listened. This time she heard a sound which filled her with fear. It was a sound like the sound which a wolf makes when it grabs a rabbit in its jaws.

"My husband," she whispered, "did you hear that?" But her husband did not answer. He did not even snore.

Slowly then, the clouds began to clear away from the face of the moon.

Put hands together in front of your face and then spread them apart as if opening a curtain.

Again the light of the moon came into the small lodge. The wife decided that she would wait no longer. Certain that this was a bad place, indeed, she crawled over to the side of the bed.

"My husband," she said, "we must leave this lodge!"

But her husband did not answer.

Storyteller: **HO?**

Very, very softly.

Audience: **HEY!**

"My husband," she said, "wake up!" She reached up and pulled his arm.

But he did not move.

Storyteller: **HO?**

Very, very, very softly.

Audience: **HEY!**

"My husband," she said and she grasped his shoulder. She felt something warm and wet! Lifting herself up on her knees she looked closer and saw that her husband's throat had been torn out!

Slowwwly, she turned to look toward the other side of the lodge. The box was open! The moonlight shone into the box! Within the box was a skeleton and the teeth of that skeleton were red with blood!

Now the wife understood. In those days when someone had been very bad in life, it was feared his spirit might wish to do evil even after death. It was common to bury such a person in a box in a small lodge away from the village. Clearly the skeleton in that box was all that was left of an evil person, and that skeleton was thirsty for human blood! Now the skeleton was content, but soon it would come out of its box and grab her and her child!

The wife thought of running, but the box was close to the door. The skeleton had only to reach out one long arm and grab her. So she spoke,

"My husband, forgive me for bothering you. I am being foolish. There is nothing for me to fear. I will go back to sleep."

Then she lay back down. But as she did so, she pulled her baby close to her. And then, slowly, slowly, no more than a finger's width at a time, she began to crawl toward the door.

Just as she reached the door, the moon went behind a cloud. All became dark and in that darkness she . . .
JUMPED UP AND LEAPED THROUGH THE DOOR.

Holding her baby close, she ran down the path towards her sister's village. She hoped the skeleton had not yet missed her, but as she ran, from behind her . . .

AAAAAARRRRRRHHHHHHHHHHHH!

The scream was more terrible than the howl of a hunting wolf. She knew the skeleton was on her trail!

She ran and ran.

Storyteller: **HO?**

Audience: **HEY!**

As fast as she could run through the forest . . .

Storyteller: **HO?**

Audience: **HEY!**

As she ran, her long hair streamed behind her. The path was narrow and the branches of the pine trees leaned in close to her. Her hair tangled on a branch. She turned back to free her hair when . . .

AAAAAARRRRRRHHHHHHHHHHHHHHH!
THERE WAS THE SKELETON RIGHT BEHIND HER, ITS LONG BONY FINGERS GRABBING AT HER HAIR!

She leaped forward and ran even faster. Holding her baby tight, she ran. She could hear the skeleton's hard bony feet pounding the earth. She could feel its hot breath on her neck. She could smell its foul breath!

Turn suddenly towards the audience and scream!

She felt as if she could run no further, but she knew she could not stop.

In front of her she saw lights and a clearing. It was the light from the fires outside the lodges of her sister's village. She took a deep breath to cry for help.

"**GOOOHHH-WEHHHH!**" she called. "**GOOOH-WEHHHHH!**"

She burst into the clearing and her legs lost their strength. She fell by the fire, clutching her baby beneath her, waiting for the skeleton's bony hands to grab her. Then . . . a hand grabbed her shoulder!

"Sister," said a familiar voice, "is it you?"

The woman looked up. People were gathered around her and her sister was touching her. She looked towards the forest path. There, cowering at the very edge of the circle of firelight, as if it feared the flames, there was the skeleton.

AAAARRRRRHHHHHHHHH!

The skeleton screamed one final time. It raised its long arms into the air. Its eyes burned with green flame! Then it turned and disappeared back into the dark forest.

An old woman came from the biggest lodge.

"Granddaughter," the old woman said, "That evil one has returned to trouble the people. Tomorrow we must go and end his bad ways forever."

When the sun rose, that old woman and many strong warriors followed the young wife to the lodge in the clearing. The old woman motioned the others to stay back and she looked into the lodge. On the bed where the husband had lain only chewed and broken bones remained. On the other side of the lodge, the lid of the box was open and in the box lay the skeleton, floating in blood.

"My friend," the old woman said, "we have only come to clear away the brush and weeds from around your lodge. Do not wake up. Do not pay attention to us."

The old woman stepped back. She motioned to the young men and they began to pile dry brush all around the house. Then they piled on sticks and logs. The old woman motioned again, and the young wife stepped forward and set fire to the brush.

Quickly the fire spread about the lodge.

Storyteller: **HO?**

Audience: **HEY!**

Now the lodge was filled with green smoke and through the open door they could see a shadowy figure moving back and forth.

Storyteller: **HO?**

Audience: **HEY!**

The old woman spoke to the young men. "Hold your clubs ready, something may try to escape."

Storyteller: **HO?**

Audience: **HEY!**

Then suddenly...**WHOOOOF!**

A GREAT BALL OF GREEN FLAME BURST OUT OF THE DOOR OF THE LODGE! Out of that ball of flame came flying a great owl. The young men swung their clubs at the owl, but it flew over their heads.

AAARRRRHHH-HOOOOOO, it called **AAARRRHHH-HOOO!**

It flew into the forest and it was gone.

To this day, if you are walking in the deep woods, you may hear that owl calling. And when a woman walks in the woods with her husband and they hear that call, she may turn to him and say, "Do you remember that story of the man who would not listen to his wife's advice?"

Storyteller: **HO?**

Audience: **HEY!**

NOTES

"The Vampire Skeleton" is a ghost story from the Iroquois Indian traditions. There are many versions of it, including one titled "The Vampire Corpse" collected in Arthur Parker's **SENECA MYTHS AND FOLK TALES**, 1923, Buffalo Historical Society. Joseph Bruchac's version places strong emphasis on the theme of men needing to listen to womens' advice -- a popular Iroquois theme. Versions of this story are told by the Tuscarora, Onondaga and Mohawk people as well.

Senjo and Her Soul

Introduction

The active participation in this story comes at the end, when the audience is left with a question to ponder, discuss, and perhaps use as a springboard for more stories. Beyond that, it is the rising sense of mystery in this engaging tale which draws the audience in to be active listeners.

NARRATIVE

AUDIENCE RESPONSE OR TELLER'S ACTION

Many hundreds of years ago in ancient China in the city of Koshu, a man named Chokan had two daughters. The oldest girl died suddenly. Chokan's heart was broken and he watched over his youngest girl with the greatest devotion. Her name was Senjo. She was exceptionally beautiful.

When Senjo came of age, many suitors asked for her hand in marriage. Chokan refused them all except for a young man who was wealthy and well respected.

Senjo was not happy. She was secretly in love with her childhood friend Ochu. Long ago they had sworn to marry.

The news of Senjo's impending marriage to another man reached Ochu. He could not bare to live in the same village where his beloved was betrothed to someone else. One night he took everything he owned down to the river to flee.

As his boat was about to leave the shore, Ochu heard footsteps. At first he could see no one in the mist. Then slowly, like a phantom, the face of Senjo appeared. She shivered in the cold night air. She carried nothing but the clothes she wore. Senjo pleaded that he take her with him.

Senjo and Ochu ran away together. They married and had two children. For ten years they lived happily in a distant village. Except, Senjo missed her father and Ochu longed for his family. One day, they decided to return to Koshu and ask their parents to forgive them and let them live in the village again.

They traveled all night in the same boat in which they had departed. In the morning they joyfully arrived in the village of their birth. Ochu went alone to Senjo's father. They agreed it would be better for him to explain what had occurred.

Chokan was glad to see Ochu. He made him flower tea and served him sweet cakes. But as the young man told his story, the old man's face grew pale. He moved his head back and forth saying, "It is impossible."

Thinking that Ochu's mind had become foolish, Chokan explained, "My daughter can not be the one you married. Ten years ago, on the night you departed, Senjo lay down on her bed, sick with sorrow. She has not opened her eyes or spoken a single word in all these years."

Ochu thought the old man had gone mad. He stood up nervously, knocking the tea cups to the floor. Saying, "I will bring your daughter and your grandchildren immediately," he rushed out of the house.

Chokan sadly made his way up the stairs. He opened the door to his daughter's bedroom. There was Senjo, on the bed where she had lain unmoving for ten years.

He leaned toward her and whispered softly, "Senjo, Ochu has returned."

To the old man's surprise, Senjo sat up delighted. She stood and put on her most beautiful robe, "Father, I am so pleased to see you. I knew you would pardon us. I could not live without Ochu. It is my fault. I begged him to take me away. You will be very happy when you meet our children."

Chokan began to shake. He could not believe his ears. He backed out the door, and ran down the stairs saying, "It is impossible."

Senjo pursued her father. The old man refused to listen to her. Frightened, he opened the door to flee from the house. But he saw Ochu walking up the path with his

daughter Senjo and two children. He turned back to the
kitchen in time to see his daughter Senjo walk toward
him in her beautiful robe, and vanish.

In China it is asked, "Which Senjo is the real Senjo?"

NOTES

This ghost story was given to me by a Zen Buddhist Nun named Myotai. She said that
it is a true story from the T'ang Dynasty based on a novel called Rikon-ki ("The Story of
the Separated Soul"). It was rewritten by a Zen Teacher named John Daido Loori and
used as a teaching tale. Zen students practicing meditation are asked this question,
"Which is the true one?"

I never give an answer to the puzzle of "Senjo and Her Soul," because I have no
answer. After the story is told, ask the audience, "Which Senjo is the real Senjo?"
Allow the question to be discussed. What is stimulating is the active discussion and
open ended relationship to a mystery.

The Vanishing Hitchhiker

Introduction

When I was growing up in North Carolina, there was a two lane highway we would take to my grandmother's house in the mountains. At one point, with mountain laurels thick on the side of the road, we would drive under an arched stone bridge. Inevitably someone would point and proclaim, "That's where that girl hitchhikes." A chill would run up my spine, and I would stare over my shoulder long after we had passed the mysterious spot.

NARRATIVE

My old friend Jill lives among the North Carolina mountains. Her home is in Hendersonville, just west of Ashville. Nearby is the Pisgah National Forest where Mt. Mitchell stands, highest mountain east of the Mississippi. The Blue Ridge Parkway winds around the mountains like a river fringed in wildflowers and evergreen trees. The sound of waterfalls tempts you to leave the road and wander among the trees. It's a wild, gorgeous part of the country.

About twenty years ago Jill's grandmother took sick. The doctors couldn't figure out what was wrong, so she had to go into the hospital outside Ashville to have some tests done. Everyday Jill's daddy would drive over to the hospital for a visit.

One night he stayed late at the hospital. I don't know if any of you have ever been in a hospital, but it's not a pleasant place to spend time. Jill's grandmamma had been there for a couple of weeks already. She was feeling kinda' down from all the tests and the uncertainty.

AUDIENCE RESPONSE OR TELLER'S ACTION

Detail of place is a major element of the urban legend and should be introduced early in the story.

Direct address is an empathy technique that identifies the audience with the real world of the urban legend.

Anyway, Jill's daddy must have stayed way past visiting hours that night, keeping his mamma company. Must have been around midnight before he left, 'cause I know they watched reruns of Twilight Zone on T.V.

In order to get home that night, Jill's daddy had to drive a short way on a major highway the State put in about thirty years ago. Everybody hated the highway 'cause they tore up the mountain layin' it down. Just as he was going down the entry ramp onto the highway that night, he saw this girl, standing by the side of the road, thumbin', hitchhiking for a ride.

Now Jill's daddy is a lawyer, so the first thing he thought to himself was that it was illegal to be hitchhiking on a major highway. The next thing he thought was that she was way too young, couldn't have been more than sixteen years old, and it was dangerous for her to be hitchin' so late at night. So he decided to give her a ride.

He pulled the car over to the shoulder of the road, threw open the passenger door and called out, "Hey, you need a ride!"

She came runnin' up to the car. She was wearin' a white party dress, kind of worn. Them mountain people, they can't afford to buy new clothes for every child that comes along, so they pass their clothes down from one child to the next until it reaches the youngest. Looked like this dress had been around for awhile. She had that kind of blond hair that's almost white. It stood out like a mist around her head in the damp night air. Over one arm she carried a white sweater, with little white pearl buttons on it, looked to be brand new.

She climbed into the car. "Yes, I do need a ride, thank you. I've been way too late at the party over to the Tylers' house. My momma's home all alone. She must be gettin' worried about me by now."

Jill's daddy is a polite man. He says, "How do you do. My name's Carlyle, Bill Carlyle."

She says, "My name's Hicks, Francine Hicks."

Now, Hicks is an old North Carolina mountain name. Just about everybody in those mountains is related to a Hicks by blood or by marriage, so Jill's daddy wasn't

Familiar, foreshadowing details help bring the listeners further in to the story.

Here the story slides to a more intimate point of view. We are no longer looking at the "friend of a friend". We begin to experience the story from his perspective.

surprised when she started directin' him up those windy roads, way back into the mountains.

He was a little worried he'd drive off the mountain into the valley on one of those hairpin turns, but he was more scared that he might end up down some dead-end road. 'Cause those mountain people, they don't trust strangers, and most of them keep a shotgun by the door.

Finally, she told him to stop. They were at the end of a dirt driveway with a wooden post with six rusty old mailboxes hangin' off it. She said, "You can let me out here. I just live up the drive."

"Oh, no," Jill's daddy tells her, "I'll drive you to your door."

"No, really, it's not far. I can walk from here. Thank you so much."

Jill's daddy watched as the girl got out of the car, and disappeared into the darkness up the drive. Then he turned the car around and drove down the mountain to his home. When he went to get out of the car he looked over on the passenger seat, and there was that white sweater with those little white pearl buttons on it. He knew that girl's family would be way too poor to replace the sweater. He was going to have to find his way back up the mountain and return it, but it was almost one o'clock by then. He decided to wait until morning and stop by on his way to the office.

He slept later than usual, and by the time he got up his family had all left for the day. He called his office to tell them he'd be late gettin' there, then he went out to the car. As he was turnin' the key to start it, he glanced over on the passenger seat, and the sweater was gone.

He looked under the seat, in the back seat, got out of the car and looked all around. He went inside, searched that house top to bottom, both floors, but he could not find that sweater. Finally, he figured he must have lost the sweater somehow, or maybe somebody had passed by and taken it. But he knew he was going to have to go back up that mountain, find that house, and offer to replace the sweater.

So he drove up the mountain. It was even scarier in the daylight, 'cause now he could see the granite cliffs dropping sheer down to the valley. A couple of times he

It is important to maintain an element of suspense, even in small details.

You might want to take a nice, brief, breath-holding pause here.

107

did end up lost on a dead end road, but luckily he didn't meet anyone. Finally, he found his way to the end of that dirt driveway, with that wooden post, with those six rusty old mailboxes hangin' off it.

Now, he didn't know which house was her's, so he parked the car at the end of the drive, got out and started walking. He stopped at the first house on the left. This was an old house with paint chipping off the boards. The front yard was overgrown with weeds and a broken tricycle lay in the grass.

Jill's daddy walked up onto the porch and lifted his hand to knock at the door. They must have been watching him out the front window, because before he could knock, the door creeeeaaaaked open.

Standing in front of Jill's daddy was a little boy, about five years old. He wasn't wearing anything except his breakfast. He looked up at Jill's daddy. Jill's daddy looked down at him and said, "How do you do? I'm Bill Carlyle. I'm looking for the Hicks' house."

The little boy didn't say a word. He just slammed the door in Jill's daddy's face. Now, Jill's daddy does not like rejection, and he has a temper. He didn't try again. He just went to the next house on the right.

This house looked a lot like the first one, except there weren't any tricycles in the yard. A rusty tractor sat off to the side. Jill's daddy went up onto the porch, lifted his hand and knocked at the door.

It took a little while, but finally he heard the sound of shoes clomping down the hall. They stopped at the front door and that door slooooooooowly opened.

In front of Jill's daddy was an old man. He was tall as a bean pole and skinny as a stick. He didn't have any hair at all on his head, but he had a lot on his eyebrows. He looked down at Jill's daddy. Jill's daddy looked up at him

Its fun, even with older audiences, to open the door with a gesture of hand from elbow out, and to make the voice sound like a rusty hinge.

As I gesture the knock with my hand, I like to pause and knock on the floor with my heel. If the audience can't see my foot, it is a very effective, eerie surprise.

The same rusty hinge sound can be made with the word "slooowly."

and said, "How do you do? My name's Bill Carlyle. I'm looking for the Hicks' house.

This old man didn't say anything either. But he pointed, one skinny, shaky finger, all the way down to the end of the drive, to the very last house on the drive. Then he closed the door. Jill's daddy walked off the porch and down to the end of the drive, to the very last house with its back to the mountains. Now this was the oldest house that he had ever seen in his life. It didn't have any paint left on the wood at all. There weren't any curtains in the windows. There weren't any screens either. It was just like two hollow eyes staring out at him. The porch roof slanted one way and the floor slanted the other.

The steps were so rotten Jill's daddy didn't trust them. He just stepped from the ground right up on to the porch. He lifted his hand and he knocked.

Knocking sound with foot again.

There wasn't any response so he knocked again, and this time he called out, "Hello. Is anybody home?" Nobody answered, so he thought maybe they were out back. He went off the porch and around to the back of the house. No one was there, but there was a clothesline with some damp, yellowed clothes on it, so he figured somebody must be home.

He went back around to the front of the house, climbed on to the porch, lifted his hand, knocked, and called, real loud, "Hello. Mz. Hicks? Are you home? I've come about your daughter, Francine."

This time he heard a slight shuffling sound. First he thought it might be mice under the porch floorboards, but it got closer and he figured out it was slippers scuffling over a rough wooden floor. They got to the front door and stopped. That door opennnnnnnned.

Rusty hinge again.

The sun was at Jill's daddy's back, so the figure in front of him was all in shadow, blocked from the light. He could just make out the shape of a tiny old woman. Her hair was like a silver spider's web on her head. She had about a thousand wrinkles on her rice paper face, and her eyes were the kind of blue that turns to water with age. She squinted up at him. He looked down at her and said, "How do you do? My name's Bill Carlyle. Are you Mz. Hicks?"

She didn't answer him, so he thought, "Well, she must be hard of hearing." He spoke again, louder. "Mz. Hicks?

My name's Bill Carlyle. I gave your daughter, Francine, a ride home last night. She left her sweater in my car and, I'm sorry, but I seem to have lost the sweater. Would you let me replace it for you?"

She said, "Francine?"

This elderly mountain woman's voice carries the sorrow and pathos of this ghost story to the heart.

"Yes, your daughter, Francine. I gave her a ride home last night, but she left her sweater in my car and somehow I seem to have lost it. Would you please just let me replace that sweater?"

She said, "Francine didn't come home last night."

"What do you mean she didn't come home? I just let her out at the end of the drive. She must have gotten home all right. Nothing could have happened to her. Look, Mz. Hicks, could I speak to your daughter? Could I speak to Francine?"

She said, "Mister, Francine died sixteen years ago today. Got run over thumbing home from a party at the Tylers' house. She ain't never coming home again."

Then she closed that door in Jill's daddy's face. And Jill's daddy, he walked down off that porch. He walked back down that driveway. He got in his car. He drove down off that mountain, and he did not ever go back.

Nice and slowly. Lots of pauses between sentences.

NOTES

This was one of my favorite ghost stories when I was growing up. It is considered by many to be the most popular of all the "automobile" legends. Certainly, there are versions of it still alive in the oral tradition all around the world. I wanted to adapt it to an area of the South that is dear to me. My daddy *did* grow up in Hendersonville, North Carolina right next to Mt. Mitchell. It is still possible to feel the presence of ghosts lurking in the shadows under the pines and mountain laurels, even if they *did* put that state highway in and tear up some of the mountain side. Also, Hicks isn't the only old North Carolina mountain name. I've got plenty of cousins, etc., in the area. There's even a "Justice Street" in one of those mountain towns.

No one has done a better job of tracing the history of this story than Jan Harold Brunvand in his classic collection, **THE VANISHING HITCHHIKER**, New York: W.W. Norton & Company 1981.

Follow-up Activities

There are plenty of good ways to follow-up the telling of this urban legend. One is to simply ask your listeners if they've heard a different version of the same story. Most have, and will be eager to share their story with you. Or, you could have them research similar stories in their area.

You might also divide into small groups, and have each group create their own legend, following the definition given at the front of this section.

If your group is shy, bring in a pile of headlines from any paper like the "National Enquirer," and let the group use these notorious urban legends as take-offs for their own. Whatever their starting point, remind your tellers that the secret should never be revealed until the <u>end</u> of the story.

Have fun.

Related Books

THE CHOKING DOBERMAN, by Jan Harold Brunvand. New York: W.W. Norton & Company, 1984.

THE MEXICAN PET, by Jan Harold Brunvand. New York: W.W. Norton & Company, 1986.

MORE SCARY STORIES to tell in the dark, by Alvin Schwartz. New York: Harper & Row, 1984.

SCARY STORIES to tell in the dark, by Alvin Schwartz. New York: Harper & Row, 1980.

TALES OF TERROR, by Ida Chittum. New York: Rand McNally & Company, 1975.

TAR HEEL GHOSTS, by John Harden. Chapel Hill: University of North Carolina Press, 1954, rev. 1980.

THE VANISHING HITCHHIKER, by Jan Harold Brunvand. New York: W.W. Norton & Company, 1981.

Old Man Daniker

This story has many forms of participation. Most notable in the style is the creation of community presence. The listener is drawn into the voices of the chorus until they seem to be part of the suspense filled conversations. See if you can identify the point at which you quit being an impartial observer, and feel as if this were your town on Halloween. For the more direct type of participation, it might be fun to have the audience join in Old Man Daniker's repetitive line, "It's goin' be a burial." You could teach this line before telling the story, or give permission for participation when it comes up during the story.

NARRATIVE

AUDIENCE RESPONSE OR TELLER'S ACTION

In Corydan, Indiana nobody went up to old man Daniker's place alone on Halloween. Old Man Daniker loved Halloween . . . too well.

A few years ago Paul and Laurie Royce, went up that hill together in the dark. It was Halloween night. They got to the top of the hill, and they were lookin' at the cornfield. Of course it was yellow, an' whisperin' kind of with the wind.

"Look at that, Paul," Laurie said.

They could see the scarecrows. Daniker had 'em all over the cornfield, and they were movin' back and forth in the wind. Paul and Laurie just knew one of those scarecrows was going to be Old Man Daniker.

Paul was in the fifth grade then, Laurie in the third, so he went ahead. "It's all right, Laurie." He went through those corn stalks until he got to one of the scarecrows that was movin. He touched it. . . it was just a scarecrow. "It's all right, Laurie, come on this way."

Laurie got kind of confused and lost in those corn stalks.

She went over by a scarecrow and she coulda sworn it was movin'. She looked up at it.

"HAPPY HALLOWEEN!"

It was Old Man Daniker! Laurie was so frightened she ran as hard as she could through that corn field to the house. There was Mrs. Daniker.

"It's all right. Come on Laurie. Come on out of there, child. You never mind my husband. He gets crazy on Halloween. Paul, you come on in here too. Now come on. I'm goin' to give you some of the fat fudge, two pieces each. Now, it's all right."

Well, they got that fat fudge and it almost made it worth it. Almost.

Daniker came into his own house 'bout 9:30 that night. He was wearing a ratty old tuxedo and there were still sticks in the arms. He had straw comin' out of the neck and the hands.

"You know I'm sick a just bein' Scarecrow Daniker out there. I want to go down the town and I want'a scare someone half to death, maybe more."

"Shut up, Clem," she said. "Look at yourself. You look like a fool. Get that straw out a' there, take a bath, and git into bed. You gotta be to the print shop early in the mornin'."

Mrs. Daniker kept a tight rein on Old Man Daniker and everybody was glad a' that. Well, she took sick in November, and she died. It was in January that Daniker started walkin' around that print shop. He does the printin' for the newspaper. They could hear him talkin'.

"Well, there's no one holdin' me back now. There's no one holdin' me back!"

Daniker used to always sit on the Liar's Bench at noon; have his lunch and his hot tea. Didn't matter how cold it was. The Liar's Bench in Corydan, it must a' been there 70 years. Coupla' years ago they tried to get rid of it 'cause they were goin' to build a buildin'. Well, there was a protest and they moved the buildin'.

Daniker's always there at noon. He was sittin' there one February day, noon, drinkin' the hot tea. Coupla' fellas sat down.

"Shhh, cold, Daniker." "Oh's gettin' colder everyday." What's headlines for tomorra?" "Are you comin' up my place on Halloween?" "What'ya talkin' about, Daniker, it's February."

"You come up my place on Halloween. It's goin' be a burial."

If you plan on having the audience repeat "It's goin' be a burial," this is a good time for a pause and slower speech for emphasis. Old Man Daniker would probably deliver the line similarly anyway.

Well, it got so nobody'd sit on the Liar's Bench when Daniker was there 'cause all he talked about was Halloween. 'Course, Bessie Meadow, the widow, she'd sit there. She'd look at him and say, "I don't scare easy, Daniker."

"That's fine, Bessie Meadow. You come up my place on Halloween. It's goin' be a burial."

Give your audience a nod this time. They should be ready to join in.

And Uncle Doctor, he went by one day. Daniker's talkin' about a burial on Halloween and Uncle Doctor leaned down and said "Well, I'll have to sign the death certificate."

"That's fine Uncle Doctor. You come up my place on Halloween. It's goin' be a burial."

They should be right with you.

Well, Daniker kept sittin' there talkin' about Halloween. Before you know it the fall had come and he's sittin' on that Liar's Bench one October day. Paul Royce, in the 6th grade now, was goin' home. The Liar's Bench was in an alley right off the main street. Daniker's got this big overcoat.

"Hey, Paul. Paul, come over here!"

"Hello, Mr. Daniker."

"I want you to take a picture of me."

"I haven't got a camera."

"I got the camera, Paul, I got a Polaroid here. Now you take it. Back up. Now wait a minute! Goin' to take this coat off."

Daniker was wearing a ratty old tuxedo underneath with straw comin' out a' the neck.

"All right, now wait, let me get the arms up. Now w-w-wait, I got to put this on."

Daniker, he picked up a pumpkin he'd hollowed out with a crazy smile on it, put it on his head.

"All right, take the picture, take the picture!"

"I got it."

"Well, you're not goin' nowhere 'til we see how it comes out. Now, come over here. Well, it's comin' out nice.

Heh, you tell your father come up my place on Halloween. It's goin' be a burial."

Play with variations on tone and speed of delivery to build suspense with the repetition.

"Well, I hope not, Mr. Daniker."

"Well, I hope so, Paul. Now good'bye."

Paul went home an' told his father what happened. His father, Fred Royce, made some calls and parents decided no one was going up to Daniker's unless they all go together and make a party of it.

Well, Halloween morning come, kids are runnin' to school down the main street. We got those gas lanterns in Corydan, still. The kids noticed that somebody'd put pumpkins on the gas lanterns with a kinda crazy smile. In the cafe people'r readin' the newspaper. On page three there was a big black border an' there was a tombstone. It said "Scarecrow Daniker."

Well, the editor, he called Daniker's house to find out who put that in the paper. "Daniker, that you?" Somebody'd picked up the phone. "Daniker? Daniker?" Whoever it was, hung up on the editor.

Word spread quick. Halloween night Fred Royce must of led sixty people, grownups and kids, up to Old Man Daniker's. The place was pitch black and Fred knocked.

"Daniker!" (knock, knock, knock) "Happy Halloween! trick or treat!"

The knocking may, of course, be done by hand on wood, shoe on floor (which makes a nice suspense if they can't see it,) or voice.

All of a sudden the place was on fire. Every room in the place was on fire! Everybody got back and the fire, it was a fierce fire. You could look in the livin' room, there musta been 30 pumpkins and they're all meltin' like they're made a' wax. Everyone's gettin' back an' back. They got the firemen up there; there was nothin' they could do, that place was burnin' too bad! They were going back an' back away from that heat. Back an' back. A little boy he tripped over. . . a TOMBSTONE! It said "Scarecrow Daniker Lies Here."

So the firemen come over and they kept diggin' till they came to it...a casket. They got the ropes underneath and they pulled the casket up.

There's the Fire Chief, Fred Higgins, "Would ya get the kids back? Would you please get the kids back! Bring the flashlights over here. All right open up the casket. Open it up. Oh my...It's Scarecrow Daniker in here. He got that tuxedo on. He got a pumpkin on his head."

Fire Chief picked up the arms, said "It ain't Daniker at all. It's a scarecrow. It's nothin' but a scarecrow here. You men, you stay here. When that fire's out I want you pokin' through it. See if you find any bones."

They didn't find any bones. Didn't know if Daniker's alive or he's dead. Nobody did.

Well, of course, November come and Thanksgiving's on its way, so everybody forgot that and gettin' busy as can be. Was Wednesday evenin'. Well, Bessie Meadow, the widow, she went out to the Baptist Cemetery, put a wreath on her husband's grave. She started to tear up little bit, took off her glasses and she thought she heard someone.

"Grrrrr-rrrrooow"

She dropped those glasses, she's helpless without 'em, so she got down on her hands and knees, she's tryin' to find the glasses, she thought she heard 'em snap.

"Rrrooowww!"

She looked up behind the tombstone. She thought this black dog was comin' at her.

"Rrrrooowww!"

And she's lookin' at Old Man Daniker's face! Well, Bessie Meadow, she made it back to town, but she spent the next month in bed. People started lookin' over their shoulders.

It was late March, cold as can be. Uncle Doctor, he came back late that night from the hospital in Louisville. He'd been at work 18 hours. He was glad to see the light on in the drugstore. It's usually closed at 10 o'clock. Uncle Doctor went in.

"Glad you're open, Russell. Aaah, 62 years old. I'm too old for these days. Ah, I know you're in the back room. I can see your shadow there. Ah, you just finish up those prescriptions an' I'll get myself one a' these cheese crackers. Then I'd like, ah, hot cup a' coffee."

Uncle Doctor went over and sat down, opened up his newspaper, got one of those cheese peanut butter crackers, ripped it open. Then he saw the coffee. It was bein' slid towards him. It was steamin' and somehow he just stared at that coffee an' he saw a man's fingers goin' right into the coffee, stirrin' it. He looked up, and there's Old Man Daniker, smilin' at him. And Daniker handed him a death certificate to sign. Uncle Doctor's frozen and Daniker just smiled and walked out the back. After that, we're all lookin' over our shoulders.

I'm in the auto parts business. I was drivin' home late one night and I take the low road. Pretty lonely. Someone was hitchhikin' so I pulled over to pick him up. All of a sudden, his hands went straight out like he was a scarecrow. I pulled that wheel and nearly hit a truck comin' the other way. I stepped on the gas. In my rear view mirror I could've sworn it was Old Man Daniker.

Halloween come around again, we're all pretty edgy. Everybody saw the gas lamps...had those pumpkins. Someone put 'em on in the night. That Halloween mornin' we're sitting in the cafe havin' coffee an somebody was readin' the Louisville Courier.

"Hey, look at this. Somethin' about Corydan, a classified ad here. It says 'one more time in Corydan, then I'm goin' town to town.' Signed O.M.D. Who you spose that is?" "It's Daniker, that's who it is. It's Daniker. It's Old Man Daniker."

"Daniker?" "Yeah, it's Daniker. The crazy old man's comin back tonight, I'm keepin' my kids in."

Not many people went out for Halloween in Corydan that night. The Royce's did. A few lively people. All the merchants, they kept everything open on the main street so there's plenty of lights. Of course there were the houses along the side streets there.

Jenny Robbins, she went out with the Royces. You know Jenny. She's 10 and got those pig tails and she's got enough freckles to cover a beach. She's a lot of fun. Well Jenny ran by the drug store, ran down the alley past the Liar's Bench 'cause she was goin to scare the Royces.

She's half way down the alley in the dark and she's leanin' against a lamppost that was all dark. An' she thought it moved. Poor Jenny, she couldn't breathe. She reached back and touched it. It seemed to be metal. Then she finally managed to turn around. Ohh, an' it was just, it was just a lamppost. She turned back. Then she saw it hangin' there. It was a man, hangin' by the neck. Jenny let out an almighty scream.

The Royces come runnin' around. Saw the figure hangin' there, twistin'. Out of the darkness someone jumped.

"HAPPY HALLOWEEN!"

It was Old Man Daniker laughin' and runnin' out the back of the alley. Disappearin' in the dark. They cut the body down. It was nothin' but a scarecrow in a ratty old tuxedo.

This Halloween, if I were you, when you go out I'd take a friend or two along, because Old Man Daniker's probably going to be in your town. Hiding behind a tree, in a ratty old tuxedo. Waiting.

HAPPY HALLOWEEN!

NOTES

I traveled to Corydan several years ago. It used to be the Indiana state capitol, and is still a lovely, lovely town. My hosts there were the Royces. I really enjoyed Paul and Laurie Royce who were in grade school then. The generosity of the whole Royce family was powerful. Walking downtown, I discovered the Liar's Bench and thought it was wonderful that people protested when they tried to move it, and moved the building instead. I fell in love with the town which was surrounded at the time by the drying October corn. Wherever you went, you could hear it whispering. I decided to make a story with the Royce's, the Liar's Bench and the corn.

JOE BRUCHAC is a storyteller and writer of Abenaki and Slovak ancestry. In his performances he uses traditional Native American instruments and American Indian sign language. He is the author of ten books of folk stories, including: **RETURN OF THE SUN**, Crossing Press; **IROQUOIS STORIES: HEROES AND HEROINES, MONSTERS AND MAGIC**, Crossing Press; **THE FAITHFUL HUNTER**, Bowman Books; **KEEPERS OF THE EARTH**, co-authored with Michael Caduto, Fulcrum Press and, **KEEPERS OF THE ANIMALS**, co-authored with Michael Caduto, Fulcrum Press, with Yellow Moon Press, Joe Bruchac has also published a tape, *Gluskabe Stories*.

SHEILA DAILEY is a professional storyteller who has performed in over four hundred schools in Michigan, Wisconsin, Kentucky, New Mexico, Arizona and Canada. She has conducted a storytelling residency at the National Storytelling Institute in Jonesborough, Tennessee. She is co-cordinator of the annual *Storytelling in Education* conference. Sheila holds a Master's Degrees in both Education and Children's Literature. Her new book, **STORYTELLING: A PATHWAY TO LITERACY**, was published by NAPPS in the fall of 1992. Her other tapes and books are available through Sheila Dailey, Storytime Productions, 1326 East Broadway, Mt. Pleasant, Michigan, 48858. Her publication, **LAND OF THE SKY BLUE WATER: STORIES AND LEGENDS OF THE GREAT LAKES**, received an extremely favorable review in the NAPPS *Journal*.

HEATHER FOREST has published two children's books with Harcourt Brace Jovanovich: **THE BAKER'S DOZEN**, which won an American Institute for Graphic Arts Award; and **THE WOMAN WHO FLUMMOXED THE FAIRIES**, which is a Junior Library Guild Selection and was chosen as a "Pick of the Lists for 1990" by the American Booksellers Association. She has toured her repertoire of world folktales for twenty years to such places as the Smithsonian Institution, the National Storytelling Festival, the Edinburgh Festival, the Milwaukee Arts Center, the Miami International Book Fair, and The World Festival of Fairytales in Graz, Austria. She has been featured at major storytelling festivals throughout the United States. She has recorded five albums of her unique blend of stories and music, with Yellow Moon Press, she has recorded a tape, *The Eye of The Beholder*.

LINDA GOSS is past President of the Association of Black Storytellers (ABS) and is the official *Griot* (storyteller) of Philadelphia. She was co-founder of the National Black Storytelling Festival. Linda Goss and Marian E. Barnes are co-editors of **TALK THAT TALK**, an anthology of African-American storytelling, published by Simon & Schuster. With her husband, Linda has co-authored a children's story, **THE BABY LEOPARD**, published by Bantam Press.

DR. FLORA C. JOY is a professor in the Department of Curriculum and Instruction at East Tennessee State University. She is the editor of the *Tennessee Storytelling Journal* . A connoisseur of Halloween stories, Flora Joy created a Halloween Storyfest program for ETSU in 1991 which drew an audience of 5,000 Halloween enthusiasts.

JENNIFER JUSTICE has been performing for close to a quarter of a century. Her work in storytelling began in 1981 when three strangers told her she should be a storyteller. Since "three" is the magic number, she took their advice. Her video, **Sharing The Circle**, was awarded the Silver Apple Award by the National Educational Film and Video Festival. Jennifer travels the country for Lesley College of Cambridge, Massachusetts teaching teachers how to use storytelling in their curriculums. She has told in thousands of schools for hundreds of thousands of children. For five years Jennifer was on the board of directors of the *Three Apples Storytelling Festival* in Harvard, Massachusetts. The *Boston Globe* awarded Jennifer Justice the title of "Master Storyteller" for her performance of stories of women who saved lives during the Holocaust.

GWENDA LEDBETTER has been a teller for twenty-five years. She was featured at the National Storytelling Festival and teaches at the National Storytelling Institute in Jonesborough, Tennessee. "Storytelling," she says, "is the best way I know of learning about this remarkable world and, most especially, about yourself." Raised on Virginia's Eastern Shore, she heard stories told at the local wharf. Once, in a boardinghouse, "A leprechaun of a man told me a story and changed my life." She studied education and voice at Queens College in Charlotte, North Carolina. In 1959 she became the Storylady at Pack Library and WLOS-TV in Asheville, North Carolina. Since 1978 she has been an itinerant storyteller, traveling across the country to festivals, retreats, schools, churches, and libraries.

BETTY LEHRMAN has been performing and teaching since 1976. She hold a master's degree in educational theater from New York University. Betty has toured her stories and songs throughout the United States, across Australia and in Thailand. A moving force in the storytelling revival, she produced the weekly family radio show, "Rainbow Tales," for seven years, and co-founded "Stories After Dark," a concert series for adults. In addition, she serves on the board of New England's *Three Apples Storytelling Festival* and teaches for Lesley College in Cambridge, Massachusetts. She has produced three audio tapes, including **Watermelon! and Other Stories**, which was winner of the *Parents' Choice Award*.

BONNIE LOCKHART is a singer songwriter based in the San Francisco Bay area. Bonnie studied Kodaly vocal music pedagogy at Holy Names College in Oakland, California, and performing arts at Reed College Portland, Oregon. Bonnie is a veteran of the Vancouver Folk Festival, the National Women's Music Festival, and recorded with the Berkeley's Women's Music Collective. More recently, she has worked as pianist and writer for the jazz quintet, Swingshift. Bonnie performs a solo show for children, "Songs and Music Games From Around The World." Bonnie appears live and on record with the song and story troupe, The Plum City Players.

RAFE MARTIN is an award-winning, internationally known storyteller and author. His work has been featured at such institutions as the American Museum of Natural History, the American Booksellers Association and the National Storytelling Festival. He is the author of a growing number of critically acclaimed books, including: **THE HUNGRY TIGRESS** (Parallax Press), winner of a 1992 Anne Izard Storyteller's Choice Award, **FOOLISH RABIT'S BIG MISTAKE** (G.P. Putnam's Sons), and **WILL'S MAMMOTH** (G.P. Putnam's Sons), both *ALA Notable* books, and his latest, **THE ROUGH-FACE GIRL** (G.P. Putnam's Sons), an American Bookseller's "Pick of the Lists." His tape, *Ghostly Tales of Japan* (Yellow Moon Press) received a Parent's Choice Award. His latest tape is *Animal Dreaming* (Yellow Moon Press).

ROBIN MOORE has been a professional storyteller since 1981. In addition to his excellent tapes, he is author of three historical fiction novels, **THE BREAD SISTER OF SINKING CREEK, MAGGIE AMONG THE SENECA**, and **UP THE FROZEN RIVER**, all published by Harper & Row. Robin recently received the *Parent's Choice Award* for his book, **AWAKENING THE HIDDEN STORYTELLER: A Family's Guide to Building a Storytelling Tradition at Home** which was published by Shambhala Publications (distributed by Random House) in 1991. To order, call 800-733-3000.

JAY O'CALLAHAN tells his original stories from Lincoln Center to Stonehenge, on shipboard and in trees. His theater performances have been acclaimed in the *Boston Globe* and *The New York Times*. A sound will catch Jay's ear and a story of fascinating depth, richness, and humanity will emerge from his imagination. Originally a novelist, Jay is recognized internationally as one of our finest storytellers. *Time Magazine* calls him "a man of poetry, wit, and elegance." His numerous and highly praised audio cassettes and videos have been published by Artana Productions.

ROBERT RUBINSTEIN began storytelling with Miss Martha Engler at the South Boston Public Library in 1965. He created and directed the nationally known Troupe of Tellers from Roosevelt Middle School in Eugene, Oregon. For two summers Robert taught at the National Storytelling Institute in Jonesborough, Tennessee. He has recorded popular tapes for children. Dodd, Mead and Company have published two young adult novels, **WHO WANTS TO BE A HERO!** and **WHEN SIRENS SCREAM**. Both of these novels have been translated into Danish. He has written over 100 articles and short stories, published in national and regional publications. In 1986, Robert received the Oregon Education Association's Noel Connall Instructional and Professional Development Award. In 1991 he produced the first "Multi-Cultural Storytelling Festival and Concert" to help foster better ethnic and racial understanding in the Eugene community.

NANCY SCHIMMEL is a storyteller/songwriter. She inherited this duel tradition from her autobiographical storyteller father and her songwriter mother, Malvina Reynolds. Nancy has performed both traditional and original stories at the National Storytelling Festival in Jonesborough, the Clearwater Festival in New York, and at festivals, schools, libraries and bookstores nationwide. Her book, **JUST ENOUGH TO MAKE A**

STORY (now in its third edition), grew out of her storytelling course at the University of Wisconsin library school. Her book, audio tape of stories and songs, *Plum Pudding*, and her video, *Tell Me A Story*, are available from Sisters' Choice Recordings and Books, 1450 Sixth Street, Berkeley, CA 94703.

LAURA SIMMS is a storyteller, poet, and teacher with an international reputation for excellence. A professional performing artist for twenty-five years, she has appeared in theaters, festivals, schools and universities in the U.S. and abroad. In 1967 she graduated from SUNY in Binghamton, New York, with honors in literature and history. Laura combines her dance/theater background with her knowledge in literature, history, myth, anthropology and psychology. A founding member of the New York City Storytelling Center, she also serves as a consultant, advisor, and board member for many institutions, including the National Association for the Preservation and Perpetuation of Storytelling (NAAPS). Her recordings include: *Stories: Old As the World, Fresh As the Rain* (Weston Woods, 1979); *Incredible Journey* (Gentle Wind, 1979); *Just Right for Kids* (Kids Records, 1984); *There's A Horse in My Pocket* (Kids Records, 1987); and *Moon on Fire* (Yellow Moon Press, 1987).

FRAN STALLINGS grew up in a storytelling family. Although trained as a biologist, she has been a professional storyteller since 1978. In her home state of Oklahoma she has reached many thousands of K-12 students through the State Arts Council's Artists in Residence program. Her nationwide workshops reach thousands more by training teachers and librarians in curriculum enrichment through storytelling. She was an instructor at NAPPS' summer 1988 Storytelling Institute and the 1991 NAPPS Congress on Storytelling in Education. In Oklahoma, Fran directs the Sunfest Storytelling Festival and is a founding member of Territory Tellers of Oklahoma. Her publications include fiction and many professional articles.

JULIA WILLIS is the recipient of a playwriting fellowship from the Edward Albee Foundation. Her work has appeared in such magazines as TRIQUARTERLY, BOSTONIA, and WRITER'S DIGEST, and the anthologies WOMEN'S GLIB, WORD OF MOUTH 2, and PLACES, PLEASE! As a former stand-up comic she writes comedy for the Boston Baked Theater, National Public Radio, and Joan Rivers. In her opinion, her cats have always been pretty remarkable beings. Okay, her dogs were nice, too.

CONTACTING CONTRIBUTORS

All of the contributors to this book are storytellers who are involved in teaching classes, leading workshops, and giving performances throughout the U.S. If you would like information on any of these activities from a teller, contact them at their address below. They will be happy to send you information on the programs and workshops they offer. Many of the contributors have produced tapes and/or records, as well as authored books (this information is provided in the individual entries above).

Joseph Bruchac
2 Middlegrove Rd
Greenfield Center, NY 12833

Sheila Dailey
Box 2020
Mt. Pleasant, MI 48804 - 2020

Heather Forest
P.O. Box 354
Huntington, NY 11743

Linda Goss
6653 Sprague St
Philadelphia, PA 19119

Flora Joy
Box 21910A
Johnson City, TN 37614 - 0002

Jennifer Justice
RR 2 - Pine Needle Rd.
Wellfleet, MA 02667

Gwenda Ledbetter
55 Beaverbrook Rd
Asheville, NC 28804

Betty Lehrman
88 Flanagan Drive
Framingham, MA 01701

Doug Lipman
P.O. Box 441195
W. Somerville, MA 02144

Bonnie Lockhart
2138 McKinley, Apt. D
Berkeley, CA 94703

Rafe Martin
56 Brighton St
Rochester, NY 14607

Robin Moore
Box 181
Springhouse, PA 19477

Jay O'Callahan
P.O. Box 1054
Marshfield, MA 02050

Robert Rubinstein
90 East 49th Street
Eugene, OR 97405

Nancy Schimmel
1639 Channing Way
Berkeley, CA 94703

Laura Simms
814 Broadway
New York, NY 10003

Fran Stallings
1406 Macklyn Lane
Bartlesville, OK 74006

Julia Willis
31 Francis Avenue
Quincy, MA 02169

FURTHER RESOURCES

There are numerous storytelling organizations, festivals and conferences around the country. We wish that it were possible to list them all, but they are to numerous to do so. The most comprehensive list of organizations and events is published by the National Association for the Preservation and Perpetuation of Storytelling (NAAPS) in Jonesborough, Tennessee. They also publish a *National Directory of Storytelling* which lists storytellers all across the U.S.. They can be reached at the address below.

Yellow Moon Press lists in its catalog over 500 books and audio tapes for all ages. In addition to our own titles, the catalog includes many hard-to-find titles by tellers from across the U.S.. Many of the titles listed in the *Notes on Contributors* are listed in our catalog. We feel it is the most comprehensive selection of storytelling materials available today. Call or write for your **free** copy of our 88 page catalog.

National Association for the Preservation and Perpetuation of Storytelling
P. O. Box 309
Jonesborough, TN 37659
(615) 753 - 2171

Yellow Moon Press
P.O. Box 1316
Cambridge, MA 02238
(800) 497 - 4385
(617) 776 - 8246 - Fax